Dear John,
Stay close to the
Master.
God Bless,
Cynthia Stewart

VOLUME 1

PRAYING PSALMS FOR AMERICA

PRAYERS FROM THE HEART OF AMERICA

Cynthia J Stewart

WESTBOW
PRESS®
A DIVISION OF THOMAS NELSON
& ZONDERVAN

Copyright © 2020 Cynthia J Stewart.

All rights reserved. No part of this book may be used or reproduced by any means, graphic, electronic, or mechanical, including photocopying, recording, taping or by any information storage retrieval system without the written permission of the author except in the case of brief quotations embodied in critical articles and reviews.

This book is a work of non-fiction. Unless otherwise noted, the author and the publisher make no explicit guarantees as to the accuracy of the information contained in this book and in some cases, names of people and places have been altered to protect their privacy.

WestBow Press books may be ordered through booksellers or by contacting:

WestBow Press
A Division of Thomas Nelson & Zondervan
1663 Liberty Drive
Bloomington, IN 47403
www.westbowpress.com
844-714-3454

Because of the dynamic nature of the Internet, any web addresses or links contained in this book may have changed since publication and may no longer be valid. The views expressed in this work are solely those of the author and do not necessarily reflect the views of the publisher, and the publisher hereby disclaims any responsibility for them.

Any people depicted in stock imagery provided by Getty Images are models, and such images are being used for illustrative purposes only. Certain stock imagery © Getty Images.

Scripture quotations are from New Revised Standard Version Bible, copyright © 1989 National Council of the Churches of Christ in the United States of America. Used by permission. All rights reserved worldwide.

ISBN: 978-1-6642-0792-9 (sc)
ISBN: 978-1-6642-0793-6 (hc)
ISBN: 978-1-6642-0791-2 (e)

Library of Congress Control Number: 2020919261

Print information available on the last page.

WestBow Press rev. date: 11/23/2020

DEDICATION

*To American Patriots and Warriors
who love America so much,
you would do anything to protect our freedoms.*

CONTENTS

DEDICATION..v
FOREWORD..xiii
PREFACE..xv
ACKNOWLEDGEMENTS...................................xix

BOOK I: INSPIRED BY PSALMS 1-41 1
Righteous Prosperity............................. 3
Our King, Our Lord.............................. 4
God Delivers 6
Rest In The Lord................................ 8
God's Favor And Blessing....................... 10
Righteous Defender 12
America's Refuge 14
Beam Upon Us 16
Saving Power And Justice........................17
Deliver Us....................................19
From Heaven's Arch 20
Everlasting Promises 21
Bountiful Blessings 22
Denounce Godlessness 23
Who Will Live With God?....................... 24
Trust His Security 25
Protect The Warrior 27
Thank You For Our Victory 28

God's Perfect Creation 30
Remember Us 32
Glorious Victory 33
Save Our Children 34
The Eternal Shepherd 36
Swing Open The Gates 37
Guide Me Lord 38
Walk Of Faithfulness 40
Stand Strong 41
You Are Our Peacemaker 43
God's Voice 44
Recovery And Relief 45
Be Strong In The Lord 46
The Joy Of Forgiveness 48
God The Great 49
The Radiance Of The Righteous 51
Your Great And Holy Nation 53
The Divine Goodness 55
America's Salvation 56
Make Haste Lord 58
Bring Your Forgiveness 59
Thank You Lord 60
God's Help And Healing 61

BOOK II: INSPIRED BY PSALMS 42-72 63
My Soul Pants 65
Lead Me To Your Holy Mount 66
You Love Us 67

PREPARE YOURSELF AMERICA	69
GOD LEADS US	70
NATIONS PRAISE YOU GOD	72
GLORIOUS STRENGTH	73
THE JOY OF WISDOM	75
BRING YOUR DEVOTION	76
PARDON ME LORD AND WASH ME CLEAN	78
JUDGE THE DECEIVERS	80
DENOUNCE THE UNGODLY	82
DEFEND US PLEASE LORD	84
A FRIEND'S TREACHERY	85
TRUST GOD ALWAYS	86
AMERICA EXALTS YOU	88
COME AVENGER COME	89
DELIVER AMERICA GOD OF LOVE	91
YOUR VICTORY OVER DEFEAT	92
GOD'S PROTECTION IS SURE	94
TRUST SONG FOR GOD	95
GOD'S COMFORTING ASSURANCE	97
PRAYER FOR OUR PROTECTION	98
BOUNTEOUS THANKSGIVING	100
GOD'S GOODNESS TO AMERICA	101
SHINE YOUR FACE	102
SING YOUR PRAISES	103
GIVE US SANCTUARY	105
WINGS OF GLORY	107
OUR ROCK AND OUR FORTRESS	108
DESTINY OF A RIGHTEOUS NATION	109

BOOK III: INSPIRED BY PSALMS 73-89 111

- Stay Steadfast 113
- Help For A Humiliated Nation 115
- The Wonder Of God 117
- Sovereign Judge 118
- Remember His Goodness 120
- Win Our Souls Again 121
- Have Mercy On America 123
- Restore America 125
- A Stubborn America 127
- Rule The Day 128
- Decimate Evil 129
- Joyous Worship 130
- Restore Your Favor 131
- Most Wonderful 132
- Joy Of Living With God 133
- If We Are No More 134
- God's Forever Promise 135

BOOK IV: INSPIRED BY PSALMS 90-106 137

- Masterful God 139
- Blessed Assurance 140
- Great Thankfulness 141
- Majestic Ruler 142
- Avenger God 144
- Obedient Worship 146
- God Righteous Judgment 148
- Our God Reigns 150
- Judge Of Truth 152

It Is His Holiness................................153
Enter His Gates..................................154
Pledge Your Integrity And Justice 155
Eternal Healing King............................157
God's Great Good................................159
Our Provider 161
Our Faithful God................................162
Confess Your Sins 163

BOOK V: INSPIRED BY PSALMS 107-150 165

Troubles Be Gone 167
Sweet Victory...................................169
Vindicate America...............................170
God's Victorious King...........................172
Works Of Wonder 173
Righteous Blessings 175
King Of Love 177
Wondrous Exodus.................................178
Worthless Idols.................................179
Always There 180
Worship Him.....................................181
Victory Songs...................................182
Glorious Law 184
The Truth-Teller................................185
God's Protection................................187
Praises From America 188
Mercy Please 189
Only You Lord 190
Precious Security 191

Joyous Harvest	192
The Blessing Of Children	194
Life In God	195
He Is Righteous	196
We Wait	198
Ever Trusting You	200
Our Eternal Lord	201
Unity Blesses	202
All Is Well	203
Almighty Goodness	204
His Love	206
Lament For Loss	207
Sincere Praise	208
Incredible God	209
Deliver The Good	211
Preserve Us From Evil	212
Persecution No More	213
Free Of The Enemy	214
National Deliverance	215
God Is Great	217
Our Great Helper	219
Caring For America	220
Universal Glory	221
God Is So Good	223
Unsurpassable Greatness	224

YOUR FAVORITE PRAYERS AND PSALMS 225

FOREWORD

Dear Good and Holy Americans,

Thanks be to God that he hears the groanings of our hearts, because for some of us, it's difficult to find the words to express all that we're feeling and thinking about our country right now.

What happened to us?
How much more can we take?
What will happen next?
Where do we go from here?

If you recognize that we are in a spiritual battle for our very existence, then *Praying Psalms for America* is just the inspiration you need to keep you focused on praying for our country. Instead of wringing your hands and groaning within your soul, you can pray with purpose.

Within these pages are prayers, beautifully written and patterned after the Psalms. Each day, author Cynthia Stewart arose to study each Psalm, and then she let the words flow. Join your prayers with hers and pray for America's hope and healing.

My greatest prayer is that you understand the urgency of praying for America. As we find ourselves at the precipice, may we make the choice to be united under the Godhead of Jesus Christ as we create a world of peace and harmony for all.

Rhonda Knight Boyle

PREFACE

The truth shall make you free.
—JOHN 8:32

I seek God's truth to guide me so I may gain deeper understanding of what is real and what is true.

The good Book is our greatest source of truth because God speaks only truth to us. As best we can, we have to block out the squawkers untethered from God's voice and hear what he has to say to us.

When I write these Psalms for America each morning, I ask God to reveal to me how to pray for us. I read and meditate on the Psalm. As I read, I think about what's happening in America. Then I let the words pour onto the page.

God gave me this idea in July 2016 when we learned our candidates for president, which, frankly, made no sense to me, based on what the media was saying about them. I turned to the Psalms and prayed for my beloved America, writing my prayers in my journal, as I've done for a decade. Since God is in charge, I asked him for insight and wisdom to understand why they were chosen. The media demonized or idolized each of them so much that I could not rely on media reports to see them for who they truly are.

As the election came around, through the Psalms, I reached great insight and understood exactly what was happening to America. I saw deception at the highest level of government, changing America into something completely different from who we are, driving agendas that don't reflect our foundational principles, and trapping our people in mistruths and ideologies that prove to be disastrous. I knew God would help us and I need trust in him and him alone.

In this devoted period, I came to understand that only a brash and belligerent soul could take on the power structures that were dismantling America. We needed someone who would come into power filled with righteous indignation, like Jesus when he kicked out those in the temple who were exploiting his faithful people. Someone who loved America and had no desire and no need to profit from this position of power to enrich his/her own coffers, in fact willing to take financial loss if necessary.

Someone who could speak the truth, regardless of whether it was politically correct or popular. Someone who would stand up for America, for our freedoms, and for our Constitution. Someone who would honor our warriors and our faithful servants. Someone who would not exploit the taxpayers and working men and women doing right by America and give them voice. Clinton? or Trump?

On December 1, 2019, I felt God's prompting again and began this same process knowing 2020 would be a highly contended race for the White House. Who would God choose for President in 2020?

I walked through the Psalms again, praying for America and wrote the prayers recorded here. I started a few months before the tragic events began in 2020 with the presidential impeachment, the Coronavirus (COVID-19) shut down, the riots, the killings, and the destruction of properties, businesses, and livelihoods. You may recognize the events that unfolded woven into the prayers.

Why the Psalms? We learn so much from the Psalms. They were shaped by people shaped by God and now they shape us. When we sing, pray, and recite the Psalms, we join voices around the world. We join the company of saints and cloud of witnesses who have found solace in Psalms for millennia.

I came to the Bible after I had my first child, though born and bred a Christian. Years later, I was prompted to engage scriptures by writing them in my own words. For the last decade I have journaled my prayers and meditations as a morning ritual.

I now realize the power of reading, meditating, and then praying scripture. I feel such incredible strength and peace from my morning time with God.

As I read each Psalm and write each prayer, I reflect the range of emotions the Psalmist expresses, especially David. The Psalmists speak frequently about fear of enemies, violence, evil deeds, etc. Even still they express their undying love and trust in God. In my prayers, my voice combines with their voices to find the fighter in me on the one hand, contrasted with the lover and disciple in me on the other.

I hope you find yourself in these prayers and make them yours.
I pray you will find solace and truth, and the answers you seek.
I pray you will find the joy of knowing God and trusting him.
I pray that you listen to God from whom all truth comes.

I appreciate you letting me share the prayers God places on my heart for my beloved America. I invite you to join your prayers with mine each day to unite in protecting the land that we love. America needs our prayers for a future safe and free!

God bless you.

In His Service,
Cynthia

ACKNOWLEDGEMENTS

This book would not have been possible without the encouragement and support of my husband Jeff. Thank you for sharing your love of Jesus Christ, the American Dream, and our beautiful family.

It is with deep gratitude I thank my mother, Maggie B., who taught me to love the Lord, to stand proud as an American, and to be a good citizen.

Thank you to my wonderful children, CrystalRose, Sean, and Gavin, and their fabulous spouses, Brett, Alixe, and Vanessa. My journey with you is the highlight of my life.

Words cannot express my gratitude to Rhonda Knight Boyle, who took this journey with me. When I asked her to post my prayers on Facebook, she not only said yes, she set up and administered our group "Praying Psalms for America." Each day she read my prayer and found a perfect picture to post with it. She encouraged me to publish these prayers and supported me every step of the way. Thank you, friend.

Where would we be without friends who encourage us. Thank you, Dr. Jorge and Gloria Gonzalez, faithful patriots and Christians, who are cheerleaders for my prayers, with lots of ideas for who needs to get this book. I am also grateful to my Facebook friends who posted "like," "Amen," "thank you," comments, prayers, and scriptures in response. Your encouragement is invaluable to me.

I extend my gratitude to my team at Westbow Press for picking up this project and helping me bring it to you!

BOOK I

Inspired by PSALMS 1-41

The first book of Psalms emphasize how <u>God comes beside us.</u>

Even though I walk through the darkest valley, I fear no evil; for you are with me; your rod and your staff - they comfort me.
—PSALM 23:4

Engaging These Prayers

Consider where God is walking beside you, giving you rest and peace, standing guard over you, or bringing you comfort. How is he doing that for America?

Let these prayers give you wisdom to these prompts:

- What experiences reveal he is beside you?
- What emotions do you feel when he's near?
- How may you pray for his presence?
- How can you pray he comes beside America?

Psalms are a collection of favorite songs written by Israelite worshippers across centuries, with nearly half of them attributed to King David. They recount experiences by humans across millennia in their interactions with God.

They are organized into five books, likely to represent the five books of the Torah – Genesis, Exodus, Leviticus, Numbers, and Deuteronomy.

At times, the topics are quite challenging when they deal with vengeance, enemies, war, tyranny, evil acts, and crimes against humanity. Though sometimes hard to engage because the despair is so real, they always recount love for God and his justice, and hope in his crusade.

My prayers may sound militant, tormented, or tortured in my attempt to channel the Psalmists' voices in light of real-world happenings, such as international aggressors, government deception, political activists, global pandemic, riots, and other such chaos. It's all happening in our world today, just as it has since the dawn of organized cultures. I want to reflect that and then turn it over to God's saving grace.

Let these prayers engage you, ignite you, calm you, free you, shape you, and lift you up in the way that God does.

RIGHTEOUS PROSPERITY

Happy are those who...delight in the law of the Lord...
In all that they do, they prosper.
—PSALM 1:1,2,3

Supreme Judge of the Righteous and the Wicked,

America knows that those in your kingdom who follow your counsel are the happy ones, for they do not descend to wicked ways, use their tongues to deceive, or belittle your believers.

America's believers delight in your righteous laws and natural order. We meditate upon your eternal Word, growing like an oak tree planted beside your living water which yields seasons of fruitfulness. In all we do, we prosper from your wisdom and guidance.

America chooses your righteous counsel. Let us not be deceived by the wicked whose ways lead to destruction. Lord, see to it that America chooses lawmakers who know and live by your righteous laws to ensure equal justice for all.

If the wicked, ill-intended, or scoffers are among them, remove them swiftly from office, like the chaff of wheat blown by the wind. For they do not govern well. They pervert our laws to erode your righteous way of life and enslave your faithful people.

Do not let the wicked have authority to judge others, nor the lawless be found in the congregation of the righteous, especially within America's halls of government, schools, businesses, and churches.

You watch over the way of the righteous within America from dawn to dusk. You ensure that the wicked and all their devious ways perish in the end. Your righteous followers will live long, happy, and prosperous lives under your watch.

Thanks be to God. Let it be so. Amen

OUR KING, OUR LORD

I have set my king on Zion, my holy hill.
—PSALM 2:6

Gracious God,

There are power-hungry leaders across the earth who conspire against America, for they want what we have created for our people. They want to ensnare us, pilfer our wealth, and destroy the American Way.

America has become powerful only because of the sacred freedoms of life, liberty, and pursuit of happiness, and because we place our trust in you. Evil leaders with unquenchable desire for power and wealth cannot create American exceptionalism.

You see it all from your high mountain and you laugh at their insolent, misguided, and ill-fated ways. You speak to them in wrath and terrify them in fury for you have set your begotten Son as king on Mount Zion.

You give all authority on heaven and earth to Jesus Christ, and he rules with great justice and love. America created this great nation by confessing you as Lord and stating publicly and pervasively "in God we trust."

As self-serving, ill-intended leaders conspire against America's believers and protectors, we ask that you reveal their evil ways to anyone trapped in their snares. Their misguided belief in themselves and the fallen angel only lead to human destruction.

Show them your fury and have your own way with them Lord. Wither them like flowers in the field under your scorching gaze. All they have built with stolen wealth will come tumbling down. Protect the believers who confess your name on bended knee.

You gave us the power to be a great nation. With your love, we saved many peoples of the world for centuries. Freedom seekers strive to live in America. Strengthen and protect all strivers, Lord, who desire the best for all.

These are perilous and shifting times as leaders of good and evil clash, with vulnerable lives at stake. Guide us on your paths of righteousness that we may bring about your kingdom on earth. With your power and authority, all people in all nations will come to know your abundant love and confess you as Lord.

Thank you, Lord. Amen

GOD DELIVERS

*You, O Lord, are a shield around me, my glory,
and the one who lifts up my head.*
—PSALM 3:3

Sovereign Lord,

In every direction there are enemies seeking America's destruction and the destruction of all that is good, wholesome, and holy. Where can we go that we don't see their evil works on display, mocking and taunting us?

They live in the unreal realms where chaos and destruction rule, and they claim you, God, are not real. They say that you will not help us. But you, Lord God, are the only thing that is real, for you alone created reality.

You are the shield around America and the believers of this great nation. You are the one who saves us, heals us, and protects us. When we cry aloud to you Lord, you answer us from your holy hill.

When we lie down to sleep, we wake again because you sustain us. Though thousands of people and hundreds of nation-states may pit themselves against America, we are not afraid, for you are with us, now and forever, to the end of our days.

America's warriors and protectors are your servants, Lord. You make them fearless, standing on the side of truth, defending the people at the heart of this great nation. There are attackers on all sides, ready to destroy it all.

They are fools Lord, bent on protecting their evil secrets. The evil ones throw trash-filled hate upon our protectors and blame the righteous for their own evil deeds. You protect our defenders because they are your warriors who set things right.

Rise up now - America beseeches you, Lord. Deliver us from the evil one's treachery. Strike down the enemy and all of his minions and break the stronghold of the wicked. America's deliverance belongs to the Lord. Our deliverance is in your hands.

May your blessing be upon your people. Amen

REST IN THE LORD

Answer me when I call, O God of my right! ...
Be gracious to me and hear my prayer.
—PSALM 4:1

Mighty God,

America prays you answer us when we call, righteous Father, for you give us shelter when we are in distress. Be gracious to us and hear our prayers for our beautiful nation.

How long will the enemies shame America and make your people suffer? How long will they love worthless things and speak deception and lies? How long will they plot and scheme in darkened rooms to overthrow America's goodwill?

How long will they run false narratives to hide the truth of their shame? How long will they promote illusions? How long will they seek to line their pockets on the backs of our workers and let the vulnerable ones lead perilous lives?

We know merciful Lord that you have set us apart for yourself, for we are faithful and honorable in your eyes. We know, gracious Father, that you hear us and respond to us when we call to you.

Believers, when you are disturbed, trembling with anger or fear, do not sin. Complain if you must but meditate in your heart and be silent. Build your case before God and wait for his verdict. Be righteous in all that you do and put your trust in the Lord.

We wait upon you for the freeing of American generations from the ravages of destructive ideas. We seek your good. Let the light of your face shine upon us, O Lord! Put gladness in our hearts at all times, just as you do in times of abundant blessings.

We will rest in you. When we lie down, we will sleep in peace, for you alone let us lie down in the safety of your arms. Come Lord come! Set all things right for our beloved America. Shield and protect us in the fight for good over evil.

Praise be to you, Almighty God. Amen

GOD'S FAVOR AND BLESSING

*For you bless the righteous, O Lord; you cover
them with favor as with a shield.*
—PSALM 5:12

Righteous God,

Bend down and give your ear to America's words and heed our distress. Hear our cries for justice Lord, for you are our Sovereign King and our just God. To you and you alone we pray at morning tide. You hear our voices, pleading our cause to you. We watch and wait for your wise instruction.

We know you God. You see all and nothing misses you. You see the wickedness so pervasive throughout our lands in places that should love justice and pursue only truth, such as in the halls of Congress, businesses, universities, and schools.

Too many elected officials and educators have become perverse in their words, duties, and actions because they have strayed so far from you. You see how they twist the Constitution and laws of our land and bend them against the honest and the brave to have their own way, Lord.

You are God, and you detest wickedness. You hate the evildoers who boast about their power, privileges, and prey. You destroy those who speak lies about you, about America, about your people, about our warriors, and about anyone working on your behalf to protect your flock. You abhor the bloodthirsty and deceitful, and they will not stand in your company.

Through the abundance of your unwavering love and justice, your beloved may enter your house. We bow down before you in awe of you. You lead us on paths of righteousness to protect and defend all that is good. Though we walk through hordes of enemies on all sides, you make our path straight and sure.

For the evil ones have no truth on their side; their hearts are bent on destruction, their throats are open graves filled with lies, and they flatter one another with their black tongues. Like the fork-tongued serpent, they twist the truth.

America prays for supernatural, biblical justice because the black cancer of deception is so pervasive and so many have trusting souls have fallen into its trap. Too many innocents are believing the lies and being deceived toward its wayward paths.

Make the evildoers bear their guilt for their many transgressions, O God, and for rebelling against you. Let them fall by their own witness to their heinous acts. Cast them out of America's Congress, universities, schools, and all arenas where they have any power to drive their perversions. Cast them out of your kingdom to a place they have no power to hurt anyone.

Let us take refuge in you, rejoice in you, O Lord, and forever sing for joy. Spread your wings of supernatural protection over those fighting for truth and justice and let them win the day. Let the people who love your name and work on your behalf exalt you, freely and openly with no fear. Lord cover us with the shield of your favor.

To you be all glory and praise! Amen

RIGHTEOUS DEFENDER

*Turn, O Lord, save my life; deliver me
for the sake of your steadfast love.*
—PSALM 6:4

God of Justice,

You turned your wrath upon America when you allowed our enemies to rule. We are bleeding from every pore. Look at our pain Lord and see that we are languishing.

The arrows of the enemy penetrate our armor and are tearing America in two. Despite the ways we are flourishing, our identity in you is being ripped to shreds.

O Lord, heal America, for our future is in the balance. How long before you bring your justice? Turn to us now and save our freedoms and righteous ways.

Deliver America, the home of the free and the brave. We are fighting for life, liberty, and justice for all who seek our shelter. America is stained, tattered, and weakened.

If we are torn in two Lord, we die. Where will your sheep turn to live a better life, if America is no more? How can our people remember you and give you praise if America is no more?

Your brave warriors have shed their blood for our just cause. Your faithful believers have risked their lives to praise you. The tears of your followers have drenched their beds.

Depart from America you evildoers, for the Lord hears the sounds of our cries. The Lord has heard our supplications and accepts our prayers.

All our enemies shall be shamed and struck with terror. They shall be turned back and put to ground. America will thrive in the love and light of the Almighty.

All glory and praise to God, our righteous defender. Amen

AMERICA'S REFUGE

God is my shield, who saves the upright in heart.
—PSALM 7:10

Lord God, Our Savior,

In you, America takes refuge; save us from all our pursuers and deliver us from the evildoers who seek to tear us apart. Cover our warriors with your shield of protection.

O Lord God, what wrong have we wrought? What harm have we caused? What have we ever taken that was not ours? Would you let our enemies invade us and leave us without a soul?

Have we not freed the masses, left our blood on foreign soil, opened our arms to refugees, welcomed our adversaries, and offered our home?

Rise up, O Lord, in your anger! Lift yourself up against the fury of our enemies. Awake, O God, for your appointed time of judgment. Let the assemblies of your people gather in your name.

Take your seat on high over all of us. You are the Supreme judge for all people. Judge America and our people according to righteousness and integrity.

End the evil and establish the righteous ones when you test hearts and minds. Be our shield and save the upright in heart. Prepare your sword and string your bow with fiery shafts for those who do not repent their evil deeds.

See how they conceive evil, are pregnant with mischief, and bring forth lies. When they dig their own pits, let them stumble and fall into the deep darkness. Return their mischief upon their own heads. Let their violence consume them.

America gives the thanks due you Lord, for your ever-present and unending righteousness. We sing praises to your holy name, our Most High God. We know you are the victorious one and we may place our trust fully in you for your peaceful reign.

Glory be to God, our bringer of peace. Amen

BEAM UPON US

*O, Lord, our Sovereign, how majestic is
your name in all the earth!*
—PSALM 8:1

Sovereign Lord,

Your majestic name fills heaven and earth!
Your glory is higher than the heavens.
You taught your children to sing of your strength, silencing your enemies, the fallen one, and all those who oppose you.

America looks into the night sky at the work of your fingers, the moon and the stars that you set in place.
Who are we that you should think about us?
Who are we that you should care for us?

Yet you made us a little lower than you God and crowned us with glory and honor.
You gave us charge of everything you made.
You put all things under our authority to care for - all creatures great and small.

You created all that is seen and unseen.
You gave America a place of honor in your kingdom to steward and to rule at your gracious hand.
You guide the lives we lead on your path of honor, glory, and truth.

Pour your sunshine into the heart of America, Lord, that we may be pleasing in your sight.
Let your rays beam through us and grow us righteous.
Give counsel to our decisions and actions in all walks of life.

Let your guiding light lead us on paths of righteousness.
Grow us in your Word that we may be good, honorable, and humble.
Let us praise and thank you eternally for all you have done.

All glory and honor are due you, our Sovereign Lord. Amen

SAVING POWER AND JUSTICE

I will give thanks to the Lord with my whole heart;
I will tell of all your wonderful deeds.
—PSALM 9:1

Our Savior, Our Lord,

America gives thanks to you with our whole heart; we tell of your wonderful deeds, how you created us - home for the brave to live free. We are grateful and exalt your holy name above all others; we sing praises to your name, day and night, our one true God.

You turn away enemies inside and outside of America. They stumble and perish before you, for you have maintained our just cause. You sit on your throne giving righteous judgment, especially for those wrongly accused for crimes they did not commit.

You rebuke nation states, evil dictators, tyrants, kingpins, crime bosses, and lawless actors - all those who want to enslave, torture, and wield evil power over your beloved people. You destroy the evil and the wicked who spread their deceptions, lies, and terrors against humanity.

You blot out their names forever. You vanish the enemies of the faithful and the righteous from ruling class. You root out and destroy their citadels, palaces, and networks and leave them in ruins. Their history perishes and disappears like dust in the wind.

Lord of justice, you are enthroned forever on your holy mount. You judge the nations with righteousness and all people with equity. You are the rescuing port for the oppressed, the falsely accused, the downtrodden, the enslaved, the tortured, and the tormented - all those receiving the blows of evil.

Rise up, O Lord! Do not let evil mortals prevail against your beloved people. We know your name and put our trust in you, for you never forsake those who seek you. When your faithful suffer, lift us up from the valley of despair, so that we may recount your praises and rejoice in your saving grace.

In God we trust, now and forevermore. Amen

DELIVER US

O Lord...you will incline your ear to do justice for the orphan and the oppressed, so that those from earth may strike terror no more.
—PSALM 10:17,18

Our Great Deliverer King,

In arrogance, the wicked persecute America's faithful warriors and defenders. Let the evil ones be entrapped by the destructive schemes they've devised. The evil one has tricked many into his wicked plans. Their hearts are lost.

They are deceived and unknowingly live his lies and do his bidding. Their desire to lead their own life apart from you has led them into paths of treachery and deceit, and lives of illusion. They do not know the truth. They do not see the truth.

They perpetuate deceitful, oppressive, and murderous practices that hurt all Americans, even our most precious babes. Their trickery evades many who are completely unaware of how they are being used and abused.

They turn goodness, righteousness, and decency on its head, enticing the poor, helpless, and unaware into their traps. They discard any thought of you. Their ways prosper for a time. They deride your beloved ones and lie from black tongues.

In their arrogance they believe you cannot take them down. They believe they will not meet your wrath. Rise up, O Lord God, and uplift your orphans and oppressed. Call your legions of angels to protect all that is good and true.

Gather your army of light workers committed to truth and righteousness. Arm your warriors to survive thousands of hateful arrows and blasphemous lies. Strengthen and call the meek to speak truth in every corner.

Deliver justice for your beloved people. Amen

FROM HEAVEN'S ARCH

*The Lord is in his holy temple; the Lord's throne is in heaven.
His eyes behold, his gaze examines humankind.*
—PSALM 11:4

Gracious Father,

America takes refuge in you.
The wicked bend their bows, fit their fiery arrows to the strings, and aim at the upright in heart.
Lord, if the foundations of America are destroyed, what future is left for your righteous ones?

We know you Lord.
You are in your holy temple in heaven's arch.
You behold all and your gaze examines humankind.
You test the righteous and the wicked.
Your very soul hates the lover of violence and deceit.

You love righteous hearts, minds, and deeds.
The righteous in America stand on your promises.
We shall see your radiant face.
Your loving arms shall embrace and welcome us.
Your peace shall reign forever.

Praise God! Amen

EVERLASTING PROMISES

The promises of the Lord are promises that are pure, silver refined in a furnace on the ground, purified seven times.
—PSALM 12:6

Our Supreme Protector,

Help, O Lord, for the wicked have penetrated every aspect our of American life. There are less and less godly ones in power.

Faithful innocent Americans are spied upon, lied about, framed, stamped on, spat upon, trampled, wounded, and killed.

The wicked utter lies with serpent tongues and double hearts. Their insatiable desire for power has overtaken their humanity.

O Lord, we pray you silence those flattering lips and boasting tongues that woo the unsuspecting with their deceitful lies.

They twist the truth to lull people into their traps to control minds. They organize crime syndicates to assimilate power.

They force their ruthless ways, caring only for themselves. They believe they will prevail and become the masters of all.

You see how they treat your beloved Americans, who abide by your laws, stand for truth, and defend what is life-giving.

You made everlasting promises that are pure, like silver purified seven times. You guard us from wicked generations forever.

No more will the wicked prowl, nefarious ways prevail, and villains be exalted in sweet America.

The future belongs to your beloved ones. America is the beacon of hope where truth reigns and the righteous flourish.

Thanks be to God in the highest! Amen

BOUNTIFUL BLESSINGS

I will sing to the Lord, because he has dealt bountifully with me.
—PSALM 13:6

Our Deliverer, Our Lord,

How long, O Lord?
Will you forget your righteous Americans forever?
How long will you hide your face from us?
How long must we be pained to the soul and sorrowful all day?
How long will our enemies exalt themselves over us?

Consider your love for us and answer our prayers!
Give your light to the eyes of your righteous ones.
Release them from the oppressor's curse.
Do not let our enemies prevail in shaking our foundations.
Raise your scepter to topple the enemy's stranglehold.

We trust in your steadfast love, O Lord.
Our hearts rejoice in your salvation.
We praise you for dealing bountifully with us.
You fulfill our destiny to be with you in your holy place.
You always fulfill your promises of peace and calm.

Your true love reigns forever. Amen

DENOUNCE GODLESSNESS

The Lord looks down from heaven on humankind to see if there are any who are wise, who seek after God.
—PSALM 14:2

Righteous God,

How is it that there are so many godless fools who believe in their hearts that there is no God? Do they not see that their life either ascends or descends at their choice?

The choice is to ascend to heaven where you rule life with love, mercy, and grace. Or, to descend to the pit where the evil perpetrator of death rules with deception, corruption, and abominable deeds.

Those living as lord of their own lives cannot resist the evil that awaits without your protection. When we give you our hearts Lord, you are our shield and our protection from all evil.

Look into the hearts of the righteous and see the Americans who glorify and worship you. Reject the perverse and the wicked so prevalent in these days.

You stand with the company of righteous Americans. You are our only refuge. America prays that you will bring your deliverance for us! You will restore your people once and for all.

We shall live in your abundant love and peace. We will rejoice and be glad in you, singing your praises all day long. Come Lord to denounce all evil and godlessness and bring us home.

We await! Amen

WHO WILL LIVE WITH GOD?

Those who walk blamelessly, and do what is right, and speak the truth from their heart ... shall never be moved.
—PSALM 15:2, 5

Father of Heaven,

Who among us may enter into heaven to sit with you?
Who may live with you, day by day, on your holy hill?
You have made yourself clear.
It is those who walk with you on your paths.
It is those who seek to live honorably and to be blameless.
It is those who do what is right according to your instructions.

They speak the truth from their hearts.
They do no evil to anyone.
They do not reproach others for their own gain.
They honor those who fear you.
They do not make gains on others' losses.
They do not take bribes to hurt the innocents.

There are blameless ones who live in America and serve others in your name. *Empower them Lord.*
There are those who seek to uphold your law enshrined in the Constitution. *Enjoin them Lord.*
There are those who take oaths of office to perpetuate what is good and true. *Embolden them Lord.*

There are those who live honorably, humbly, and even sacrificially to help others. *Enliven them Lord.*
There are those who walk the long and narrow path into your kingdom. *Educate them Lord.*
There are those who live in your image according to your precepts. *Enlighten them Lord.*

To you we give all gratitude and praise. Amen

TRUST HIS SECURITY

*The boundary lines have fallen for me in pleasant
places; I have a goodly heritage.*
—PSALM 16:6

Father God Protector,

Spread your wings across America, Lord, for we look to take refuge in you.
We knew from our beginnings that you are our Lord.
Apart from you there is no good that can happen.
You are the creator of good; all good comes from your hand.

Those of us who kneel before you are honorable and noble.
You delight in us Lord.
You welcome us into your loving arms.
You speak words of love with our name upon your lips.

We choose you and only you Lord.
We accept our portion from you with praise for it fills us.
You direct our future and supply all our needs.
Our heritage in you is good!

We bless your holy name and revere your holy counsel.
We listen to our hearts where you have made your home.
We keep you always before us and all around us.
We feel secure, protected, and hopeful with you here.

The hearts of America rejoice that our people thrive.
America is the land that we love and call home.
Your faithful ones are shielded by righteous laws and leaders.
You will never give us up to those who would harm us.

Light your path of life for us Lord.
Be present with us and multiply our joy.
Secure our blessed future.
For in you we trust forevermore.

Thank you, Gracious Father! Amen

PROTECT THE WARRIOR

By your sword, deliver my life from the wicked.
—PSALM 17:13

Savior God,

Hear the just when Americans speak and attend to our pleas.
Bend low and give ear to our prayers from lips free from lies.
Vindicate us, Lord, for your eyes see only what is right.
You see the evil ways of those who bow to your adversary.

Our warrior is accused wrongly and falsely.
Test his heart in your nightly visits; see if there is any falseness.
You made him brash, vocal, and loud to call out the deceivers.
The persecutors are unjust and irrational in their crusade.

They are on a mission to destroy the warrior.
Strengthen his armor, keep him steadfast, do not let him fail.
Incline your ear to our prayers, O God, and hear our words.
Your ways are just, righteous, and true.

Give refuge to the warrior and those with him.
Shield him from the adversary's lies, deceptions, and evil ways.
Guard him as the apple of your eye.
Hide him in the shadow of your wings from evil strivers.

Close innocent ears to lies and tune our ears to your truth alone.
Leave the wicked ones empty-handed in their futile haunts.
Rise up with us to confront and overthrow them.
By your sword, deliver the just from the wicked.

Let us praise and glorify you, our Savior, for delivering us. Amen

THANK YOU FOR OUR VICTORY

He delivered me because he delighted in me.
—PSALM 18:19

Lord of Victory,

You are America's strength, steadfast and true.
You are our stronghold in whom we take sanctuary.
You are our protection and safe haven, our refuge in trouble.
We call for you Lord and praise your worthy name.
We trust in you to save us from the enemy and his evil doers.

Though death may wrap its knotty cords around us,
When the destroyer sends violent winds to blow us away,
Or when the roots of the evil entangle us,
Or when the snares of death rise up to consume us,
In our distress, we call upon you Lord and cry for help.

From your sanctuary you hear our voices.
Nothing misses your ears, tuned to our every need.
In your anger, you rock the earth to its very foundations.
The mountains tremble and quake.
The volcanoes erupt and seethe their fiery lava.

Your anger sends forth the fire of heaven to purge the evil.
You make yourself known to the attacker,
Exhaling smoke from your nostrils,
Expelling fire from your mouth,
Flaming forth coals from your piercing eyes.

You descend from your throne, flying on the wings of the wind,
Thundering the heavens with your voice,
Scattering the enemy into every direction.
You draw us into your protective arms.
You deliver us from the clutches of death.

O Lord, your way is perfect, and your promises are true.
You are our rock and our salvation.
You give victory over all to your anointed ones.
For this, we raise your glorious name on high.
In jubilant victory we dance and sing your praises.

In God we trust. Amen

GOD'S PERFECT CREATION

*The heavens are telling the glory of God; and the
firmament proclaims his handiwork.*
—PSALM 19:1

Glorious Father,

America lives under the heavens revealing your glory.
We sit under the skies proclaiming your handiwork.
Nature in its splendorous ways pours out abundant life in witness of your plentiful supply.
In the slumber of night, all knowledge is declared for our benefit within our lofty dreams.
Eternal proclamation of God's glory extends to the ends of the earth, by day and by night.

The sun steps out of heaven's canopy, like a beaming bridegroom from his wedding tent.
Like a champion, it runs its course with strength and power.
It rises from the apex of the heavens and circuits to the end.
Nothing is hidden from its heat and its healing light reveals your vast reserves.
Under its healing glow, all things grow and thrive.

Your law is perfect for it revives our soul.
Your precepts are right for they help our hearts stay pure.
Your commandments are clear and enlighten our eyes to see.
Your ordinances are true, bringing equity and justice to all.
Fear of you is righteous, guarding and protecting our paths.

America is wise to base our laws upon yours.
Her people are eternally rewarded to live according to your ordinances, precepts, and commandments.
For you Lord revive our souls, rejoice our hearts, enlighten our eyes, purify our beings, and make us righteous.
In your glowing love, we grow happy and strong.
In your righteous way, we find peace and calm.

Your presence is more desired than the finest gold.
Your love is sweeter than the sweetest honey.
You detect our errors, clear our faults, and fend off wrongful domination for us.
You separate us as blameless from our transgressors.
O Lord accept our heartfelt vows and our prayerful meditations.

Glory to God, our Redeemer King. Amen

REMEMBER US

May we shout for joy over your victory, and in the name of our God set up our banners.
—PSALM 20:5

Lord and Savior,

May you answer America in time of trouble!
May you protect us in the name of the God of Jacob!
May you send help to us from your sanctuary,
And give us your support from Zion.
May you grant us victory in your name.

May you remember all of our offerings,
And regard with favor all that we have sacrificed.
May you grant our heart's desire and fulfill our plans.
May we shout for joy over our victory in your name.
May you fulfill all our petitions.

O Lord, we know you will help your anointed.
Answer from your holy heaven with mighty victories.
We take pride in the name of the Lord our God.
The enemy will collapse and fall, and we shall rise and stand upright.
Give freedom to America, O Lord; we pray you answer us.

Thank you, Lord. Amen

GLORIOUS VICTORY

*In your strength the king rejoices, O Lord, and
in your help how greatly he exults!*
—PSALM 21:1

Victorious God,

Americans rejoice in your strength, O Lord; and we exalt you for your help!

You fulfill every longing within our hearts; and do not withhold your righteous purpose.

You meet us with the richest blessings, direct from your hand.

You set the Statue of Liberty in our harbor as a beacon of freedom.

When we asked to become a nation, you made us one, to live forever free.

You made us beautiful, full of your splendor from sea to sea.

You bestow never ending blessings upon us.

You uplift us with your presence, giving us endless joy and hope.

We have made "in God we trust" our motto, to glorify you in all things.

Our enemies are your enemies, for they live and breathe lies; our haters are your haters, for they disdain your majesty.

You consume evil doers with the fire of your righteous indignation. Their offspring will be blotted from humankind.

No longer will their evil plans against America and against you succeed. No more will their mischief find its victims.

You expose them, putting them in your scorching light. You convict them with your arrows of truth, revealing who they are.

We exalt you on high Lord. We sing our praises and celebrate your mighty power.

Great is your faithfulness. Amen

SAVE OUR CHILDREN

...He did not hide his face from me but heard when I cried to him.
—PSALM 22:24

Almighty God,

America's stolen young are crying out in distress.
They are targeted and forsaken, used and abused.
They are torn from their mothers' breasts,
From the loving arms of their families,
Rendered an unwanted and inhumane life,
Their cries and misfortunes wrench our hearts.

Have you forsaken them Lord?
We commit our cause to you.
We pray that you mount your army of soldiers,
Raise up your legions of angels.
Our requests are urgent and relentless to save the children Lord!
Stop these evil deeds against our innocents.

No more trafficking, stealing lives, or abusing children.
No more Lord! No more!
You are our God, our greatest defender.
You weep at the destruction of human life.
Come quickly Lord to aid and defend these little ones.
Save them from the mouths of lions who rip out their innocence.

Shield them and give them their lives free of violence.
Free them to live out your plans set before them.
Give them all the days of their lives with their loving families.
Great defender, we praise you to the end of our days.
We praise you among all the nations.
Hear our cries, save our young, and reveal your glory.

You have promised days when all the ends of the earth shall remember you and turn to you.
All families shall worship you.

Dominion belongs to you and you alone rule over all nations.
Shelter your precious ones in your loving protective arms.
We proclaim your deliverance for all your children.

Save us Lord. Amen

THE ETERNAL SHEPHERD

The Lord is my shepherd; I shall not want.
—PSALM 23:1

O Lord,

You are America's great provider, offering your bounty from your loving hands.
You are our comforter, giving us rest in green lush pastures to soothe our souls.
You are our loving guide, leading us beside living waters to give us peace.
For your name's sake, you lead us on the right paths directly to abundant living.

Though we may walk in the darkest valley of despair and death,
We have no fear of the lurking darkness.
For there you are, right beside us, holding our hands.
You carry your sword and your shield to protect us in every situation.

You prepare a living feast for us, inviting us to your table of plenty.
We eat comfortably in the presence of our enemies, for you sit with us, assured and in charge.
You anoint our heads bowed before you with oils of gladness.
Our cup of your abundance and grace overflows.

All that is good and true, you give to us out of your love for us.
You invite us into the mansion you built for us to live in eternity's embrace.
You call us to a life of mercy and grace in our forever home.
There we may bring generation after generation of our beloved people, our patriots and our warriors, our free and our brave.

Praise be to our eternal Shepherd! Your peace reigns supreme!
Amen

SWING OPEN THE GATES

Who shall ascend the hill of the Lord?
And who shall stand in his holy place?
—PSALM 24:3

Lord of Hosts, King of Glory,

America is the Lord's; all of it and everything in it;
Those who live here are yours Lord,
For it is you who established this nation.
It is you who called people from across the seas.
It is you who is the creator of America.

Are we welcome before you, God?
May we rise to your holy mount?
Will we stand in your holy presence?
You call your servants with pure hearts;
Those who believe rightly and bow only to you.

America has hard-won integrity, genuine devotion, and single-minded God-given purpose.
Because you are the God of salvation,
We receive your blessings and righteous vindication.
In the company of believers, we seek you Lord,
We seek your face, the God of Jacob.

Lift up your hands America and open the doors to your hearts!
Swing open wide your gates for eternal freedom to come in!
Welcome your King of glory, your one true God,
The King of glory, your strong and mighty Lord,
The King of glory, the Lord of Hosts, on his saving mission!

Praise God in his glory! Amen

GUIDE ME LORD

*Lead me in your truth, and teach me, for you are the
God of my salvation; for you I wait all day long.*
—PSALM 25:5

Father God,

To you we lift up our souls; for in you and you alone we trust.
Do not let anyone twist our good deeds as somehow shameful; or let
our enemies dominate us.
Do not let anyone shame those who confess you as Lord; shame only
the wanton traitors.

Good and upright are your ways, O Lord.
Help America know your ways;
Humble us and teach us what is right.
Lead us in your truth, for only your truth is real.
Help us remain faithful to your covenants and decrees.

Forgive our guilt from the misguided actions of our youth.
Remember your mercy and enduring love from times gone by.
For you and you alone are the God of our salvation;
We seek you and wait for you, day in and day out.
Remember America, for your name's sake, O Lord!

The humble shall abide and prosper in your love;
Our children shall grow in wholesome ways.
You shall befriend those who revere you;
And make your covenant promise of eternal life known to them.
Keep our eyes turned to you, never to look away.

Pluck our beloved ones out of pain and distress;
Relieve our affliction and trouble;
Forgive our hurtful sins and mistakes.
Guard us, Lord, from those who violently hate you.
Deliver us and preserve our integrity that we may live true.

Redeem America from the snares of the evil one,
That we may remain in your favor forever.

Praise Almighty God! Amen

WALK OF FAITHFULNESS

*For your steadfast love is before my eyes,
and I walk in faithfulness to you.*
—PSALM 26:3

Gracious Lord,

Vindicate America! We have led the world with integrity,
Because we were founded upon your trustworthy laws.
Examine our resolve in staying true to you.
Test your humble followers in heart, mind, and spirit.
See our faithful walk guided by your steady hand.

Do not let us be deceived by worthless hypocrites;
For we hate being in company with the evil one's pawns.
We will not abide their wicked ways.
Do not let us lose our purity to their bloodthirsty bribes.
Do not let us be swept away with sinners.

Cover your faithful ones with humility and resolve.
We kneel at your sacred altar,
Singing songs of thanksgiving,
Recanting stories of your wondrous deeds, and
Telling of your majestic house, the glorious abode we call home.

Let us walk steadily in your integrity;
Supply your mercy and grace to cover us.
Let us stand our ground for righteousness and justice.
Add us to the great congregation, O God,
To sing praises for your abundant blessings.

In God we trust. Amen

STAND STRONG

The Lord is my light and my salvation; whom shall I fear?
—PSALM 27:1

Dear Lord,
You are the saving light for America!
Whom shall we cower to that is lower than you?
For we can hold onto you forever, fearing no one.
We can raise you above all others, kneeling to no one.

There are enemies inside and outside our cities.
They seek to attack and destroy America.
Even these evil pawns will tremble and fall before you,
For you do not allow our adversaries to overrule us.

When our assailants threaten war,
Our righteous hearts remain strong.
We muster our courage to meet them head on.
We stand our ground, for your heavenly armies are with us.

Cover us in the shelter of your arms in days of trouble.
Conceal our vulnerable ones with your wings of protection.
Set us far away from trouble,
High on the mount nearest to you, Lord.

We will be high above the encroaching enemies.
There we will give you praises for our freedom.
We will sing joyously of your inscrutable ways.
We will dance to the glory of life with you.

America asks this of you, Savior King,
That we may live in the home of your protection and blessing;
So that day after day we may behold your beautiful loving eyes,
And gain wisdom from your unparalleled wisdom.

Make America the land where only your good prevails.
Trust in the Lord, America.
Be strong and let your heart take courage.
Trust in the Lord!

For God is true to his promises! Amen

YOU ARE OUR PEACEMAKER

To you, O Lord, I call; my rock, do no refuse to hear me, for if you are silent to me, I shall be like those who go down to the Pit.
—PSALM 28:1

Prince of Peace,

It is you, our greatest defender, whom America calls.
Listen to our pleas Lord, and do not close your ears to us.
When you are silent, it's like living in the darkest hole.
Hear our voices, our supplications, and our cries for help.
See our lifted hands, our lifted eyes, and our lifted hopes.

Don't let us be dragged into wicked company;
Into the lairs of those who work for the evil one;
Or listen to those with double tongues, speaking peace,
While doing evil deeds in secretive places.
Give them their due according to the evil work of their hearts.

Blessed are you, Lord, for hearing the sound of our pleadings.
You are America's strength and our shield.
Our hearts trust in you alone.
You help us and we exalt you.
We sing our praises and thanksgiving to you.

You are the Lord and the strength of our people.
You are the saving refuge for your anointed within our lands.
You save our people because they are yours.
You bless our heritage offered from your hand.
You shepherd us and give us a future of blessedness.

All praise and glory to the great peacemaker! Amen

GOD'S VOICE

> *The voice of the Lord is over the waters, the God of glory thunders, the Lord, over mighty waters.*
> —PSALM 29:3

Almighty God,

There is no rival in America for your authority and power.
We testify to your glory and strength over all things, even the heavenly beings who accompany you.
The glory of your name is unmatched.
We worship your absolute power and holy splendor.

At your voice, the sun breaks to bring all things into your cleansing light.
At your voice, flames of fire flash forth to purge corruption.
At your voice, the cities and the wilderness shake, dismantling oppressive structures.
At your voice, the evil ones flee only to find themselves face-to-face with your piercing gaze.

You sit enthroned over America, its mountains and valleys,
Its highways and byways, and its heart and soul.
There is no King above you,
No power greater than you, and
No command fulfilled that isn't yours.

May you give your people throughout America your strength.
May you bless your people with everlasting freedom!

And so, it is. Amen

RECOVERY AND RELIEF

...Weeping may linger for the night, but joy comes in the morning.
— PSALM 30:5

Gracious Lord,

America praises you for you have restored us from near death.
You gave no time for our enemies to rejoice over our suffering.
We cried out to you for saving grace and you healed all of our afflictions.
You breathed life back into our souls, raising us from death's clutches.

Sing your praises America, for our faithful One.
His angry flashes will last for an instant, but his undying love lasts forever.
Though you may weep through the night, his joyous countenance greets you every morning.
The Lord faithfully restores his beloved ones.

Even in our prosperity, Americans know you are our source and we shall stand firm in you, Lord.
By your favor, you established us as the leader among nations.
We turn to you in all situations, in our distress, and in our prosperity,
For you hear our supplications and answer our prayers.

Let our foundation in you never crumble.
Who will stand firm in proclamation of you if we are no more?
Let us never fall from your grace.
Who will fight freedom battles around the world if we are no more Lord?

You and you alone may transform our sorrow into happiness.
Only you can cloth us in joy, so that we may praise you with loud and beautiful melodies.
America, give thanks to God, forever and ever.
For he is our only hope for salvation.

All glory be to God. Amen

BE STRONG IN THE LORD

...Be a rock of refuge for me, a strong fortress to save me.
—PSALM 31:2

O Lord,

America seeks refuge in your righteousness.
Deliver us from anything that could harm us.
Incline your ear to hear our prayers and rescue the vulnerable.
Be our fortress where our people may seek your shelter.

Lead us on right paths to reflect your goodness.
Shield us from hidden networks of deception and lies.
Commit our spirit into your hand, like our Lord Jesus.
Redeem your faithful ones, our Lord of saving grace.

You hate those who idolize worthless things.
Let our people not be among them.
Though we have adversities and afflictions,
Your grace is sufficient to cover them.

Deliver your full healing for our people in distress.
Mend us in all our broken places; give us your mercy.
Confuse the plans of those who plot our destruction.
Protect our freedoms from adversaries craving to enslave us.

We trust in you, O Lord, for you are our God.
Our life as a nation is in your hands.
Beam your loving light across our lands.
Save all that is beautiful with your steadfast love.

Silence the lying lips of those speaking contempt.
Put the wicked to shame in your public courts.
Dumbfound the evil doers stealing our innocents.
Open the eyes of the vulnerable to see your truth.

Your goodness is abundant for those who revere you.
Your protection is impenetrable for those you shelter.
Your grace is transcendent for your beloved ones.
Your love is unwavering for your choice ones.

Love the Lord with all your heart.
For the Lord preserves the faithful.
Be strong in the Lord and let courage win your heart.
Wait upon the Lord for your just rewards.

Thank you, God, our Rock and our Redeemer. Amen

THE JOY OF FORGIVENESS

*Many are the torments of the wicked, but steadfast
love surrounds those who trust in the Lord.*
—PSALM 32:10

Merciful Lord,

America is happy when you forgive our transgressions,
Cover our sins,
Impute no iniquity,
And clean our spirit of any deceit.

When we stay silent in regard to you or edge you out,
Our integrity wastes away and our identity slips away.
We lose our grip on what is real and what is true,
Our strength weakens, and we lose our grasp on who we are.

When we acknowledge our sins to you,
Reveal our failings,
Confess our transgressions,
You forgive our guilt and redeem us, Sovereign Lord.

Therefore, let us offer faithful prayers to you,
Then, though stormy waters approach our shores, they cannot drown us.
You provide our shelter and preserve us from trouble.
You surround us with joyous freedoms of your saving grace.

You promise to instruct us and teach us your ways.
You counsel our every decision and keep your watchful eye upon us.
You ask that we not be stubborn to avoid you or unbridled to reject
you, so that we may stay the path, ever close to you.

The wicked lead torturous lives where joy goes missing.
The steadfast trust in the Lord and share his abiding love.
Stay with us Lord, that we may rejoice in your righteousness, and
that we may shout joyously from our hearts of gladness.

Praise God! Amen

CYNTHIA J STEWART

GOD THE GREAT

Rejoice in the Lord, O you righteous. Praise befits the upright.
—PSALM 33:1

Omnipotent Father,

America, rejoice in the Lord always, rejoice.
Praise his benefits with your singing and dancing.
Sing choruses to him with guitars and tambourines.
Make beautiful melodies for him with your harp.

See his promises and his truths painted on the skies.
See his love for justice freeing slaves and protecting innocents.
See his healing grace, bringing miracles to the infirmed that they may walk again.
Where can you look that his glory does not reign?

From the words of his mouth, the heavens were made.
From his breath, he created all things.
The roaring waters he called into seas,
And gave borders to the prospering lands.

America, stand in awe of your Lord.
For his Word is trustworthy.
His ways are righteous, guiding us to love-filled lives.
His commands fulfill their destiny.

Though nations sit in counsels and plot the world's fate,
They plot in vain without the Lord's power.
The Lord's counsel stands throughout eternity.
His love thoughts pass through all generations.

America is a happy nation pledged to God.
So are all other nations who turn themselves over to him.
His inheritance remains forever.
His ways stand the test of time.

The Lord sees all from his heavenly throne.
No one misses his gaze; everyone is under his scrutiny.
No principality can stand against the Lord.
No power-hungry evil doer can survive God's wrath.

He keeps his eyes on those who worship him,
On those who keep his holy commands,
On those who hope in his forever love.
That he may give them life eternal.

America, seek the Lord.
He is our only hope for a future.
Be glad in him and trust his holy name.
Love us Lord for we place our hope in you.

Your name is praiseworthy always. Amen

THE RADIANCE OF THE RIGHTEOUS

Look to him, and be radiant; so, your faces shall never be ashamed.
—PSALM 34:5

Our Beloved Lord,

America, bless the Lord at all times, and praise his holy name with every breath.
The cherished souls of America receive gifts from the Lord.
Listen humble ones and be glad in him.
Let us magnify the Lord and lift his name on high.

When we seek the Lord, he answers us.
He delivers us from his adversary in answer to our prayers.
Let his love light shine brilliantly through our faces, so we will never be ashamed.
When America cries out to save the distressed, the Lord hears and saves each one from torment.

The Lord is present, and he delivers us because he loves us.
Taste his all-encompassing beauty and see that the Lord is good.
He makes America radiant when we take refuge in him.
He fulfills every need for those who revere him and pursue his righteousness.

Those who suppress his name and harm believers,
Always suffer his wrath,
While those who seek the Lord receive good from his hands.
Come, listen to the wisdom of our awesome God.

Do you desire a full life and many days to enjoy good?
Then do not speak evil thoughts or deceive anyone.
Avoid all evil acts and do only what is pleasing to the Lord.
Seek peace in your heart and pursue it with every action.

Love the Lord God with all your heart.
The eyes of the Lord behold the hearts of the righteous,
He hovers over the broken hearted, lifting their spirits.
His face turns away from evil doers, erasing their harm.

When we suffer afflictions, the Lord rescues us.
He frees his beloved from brokenness and destruction.
He consumes evil ones by death, their souls condemned in fire.
He redeems his servant nation America from condemnation to live eternally with him.

Thank you, Lord. Amen

YOUR GREAT AND HOLY NATION

*Contend, O Lord, with those who contend with me;
fight against those who fight against me!*
—PSALM 35:1

Majestic Lord, Our Rock and Our Redeemer,

Rise up with America's warriors to fight those who seek harm.
Bring your shield and your arms.
Calm our souls and be our salvation.

Put the enemy to shame; scatter those who seek destruction.
Confuse them, turn them back, and drive them away.
Let them slip into the dark and horrid pit they've made.

Though we did not pursue them, they pursued us.
They repaid our acts of kindness by killing our servants.
They killed our people and planned more destruction.

With your help, we found their web of planned attacks.
With your help, our warriors fought their leaders.
They ensnared themselves in the nets hidden for us.

America, let your souls rejoice in the Lord!
Exalt his deliverance from all treachery and evil plans.
Who is like the Lord?

Who else delivers innocents from the evil one's snares?
Who else frees the trusting from those exploiting them?
Thank the Lord and sing praises to his mighty name.

Be close to us, Lord, when days of dread threaten.
Ready your defenses for planned attacks against us.
Cover our warriors with your shield of protection.

Let no defenders fall at the hands of the destroyer.
Vindicate our good works, and let our peace prevail.
Shame and confuse those working to take our freedoms.

Lord, awaken those who fight against us to see you're with us.
Our defenders fight to bring freedom for the downtrodden.
You made our peaceful nation where freedom rings.

They fight evil plans of those corrupted by power and privilege.
They fight under your banner and your shield.
They fight with your love and your honor.

Let us bring peace across the nation and the world.
Let us bring freedom to worship you everywhere.
Let us bring love as the community of loving persons.

Let us fulfill your plans to bring all people under you.
Let us fulfill your destiny of salvation.
Let us be your great and holy nation.

Great is the Lord who perpetuates the well-being of his servants.
Amen

THE DIVINE GOODNESS

Your righteousness is like the mighty mountains, your judgments are like the great deep; you save humans and animals alike, O Lord.
—PSALM 36:6

Compassionate Lord,

Evil ideas entice America's enemies deep in their hearts.
They have no fear of you for they cannot see you.
They see only themselves, and flatter themselves unceasingly.
They believe their wicked acts are hidden, never to be seen.

All the words from their mouths are deceitful lies.
They always act in self-interest and nothing they yield is good.
They plot hurtful acts upon America's peaceful souls.
They descend further into evil's realm as they perpetuate harm.

Perish the arrogant who tread on our freedoms.
Silence deceitful liars who entice the trusting away from you.
End the wicked harm to your beloved ones.
Save your created ones who turn to you for salvation.

Your righteous judgments stand mighty like our mountains,
For your verdicts extend justice around the globe.
Your faithful protection is like the clouds covering our skies.
Your steadfast love for us extends through heaven's gate.

You set a welcoming feast before us in your mansion.
Your draw drink for us from the river of your abundance.
You offer the fountain of life from your eternal stores.
In your glorious love light, we see our magnificent future.

Seal America's fate with yours forevermore. Amen

AMERICA'S SALVATION

For those blessed by the Lord shall inherit the land,
but those cursed by him shall be cut off.
—PSALM 37:22

Sovereign Lord,

America has funded protection for nations across time.
We are generous with our resources for all in need.
We turn your blessings into good for all people.
We shall inherit your provision in your eternal home.

You hold us by the hand to help us walk secure.
You guide us on righteous paths to be right with you.
You show the way to everlasting peace.
You delight in us when we stay faithful to you.

America has held onto you, our true source, through the years.
You have never forsaken your faithful or left children begging.
We continue to give liberally, lending aid everywhere.
We grow our children to be a blessing to the world.

We have learned from you that we may enjoy your everlasting love
and walk daily with you.
We uphold your righteous cause, for you love justice.
You will never forsake us if we never forsake you.

Though wicked nations plot to kill Americans,
And to destroy our sovereign lands,
You will never abandon us to their wicked power,
Or let our defenders be condemned if brought to trial.

Though we witness the oppressive acts of the wicked,
Towering over their victims,
In time, the righteous ones will see them no more.
Their heinous acts stripped from all memory by you.

CYNTHIA J STEWART

America, stay with your peace agenda for the world.
Don't give up hope, for the Lord gives posterity to the peacemakers.
He ends the ill-gotten reign of terror and wickedness.
Cutting off its future for generations to come.

America's salvation is straight from your hand Lord.
Give us strength, give us power for good, and give us protection in battle.
Help our warriors and rescue our innocents.
Save your people forevermore.

Be our victory triumphant, Lord. Amen

MAKE HASTE LORD

O Lord do not rebuke me in your anger or discipline me in your wrath.
—PSALM 38:21

O Lord,

Do not turn your eyes away from America in our time of need.
When we are jeered at or attacked, please defend us.
When our enemies lay snares for us, show us the way out.
When they speak of ruining us and meditate on treachery against us day in and day out, protect us.

America waits for you Lord, for we know you always answer us.
We pray to you on bended knees knowing you are our protector.
We repent our transgressions and our sins, with sorrow and contrition.
We seek to do good, bring peace, and lead the world in freedom acts.

Do not be far from us Lord.
Make haste to help us.
You are our stronghold.
Bring your shield of righteousness and justice.

We praise you, our Lord and our Savior. Amen

BRING YOUR FORGIVENESS

*You have made my days a few handbreadths; and
my lifetime is as nothing in your sight.*
—PSALM 39:5

Gracious Lord,

America, guard your ways and do not sin with your tongue.
Be quick to listen and slow to speak when the wicked are in your presence.
Be silent, be still, and hold onto your peace.
Let the Lord of wisdom lead your thoughts and words.

Only the Lord knows the end times.
Our days are fleeting and only he can measure our worth.
We may gather and heap up goods, but to what end?
Only acts of righteousness live in eternity.

America places our hope in you, gracious Father.
Listen to our prayers and consider our pleas for forgiveness.
Send peace into our hearts that we may live and lead well.
Give us your continued blessings that we may spread your goodness.

Praise God. Amen

THANK YOU LORD

*He drew me up from the desolate pit, out of the miry bog,
and set my feet upon a rock, making my steps secure.*
—PSALM 40:2

Merciful Father,

You inclined your ear to America, waiting patiently for you.
You drew us up and set us securely upon your rock.
You put a new song in our heart to praise you.
Others will hear of your merciful acts, so abundant.
Happy are those who trust in you and idolize none but you.
You multiply your wondrous deeds for us.
None can compare to you, Father of all blessings.

You have no desire for sacrifices or sin offerings.
You desire that we love you and gather everyone in your name.
We set our laws upon your laws and delight in doing your will.
We seek your peace and pursue peace talks globally.
We tell of our deliverance in the great congregation.
We share how faithfully you protect your beloved ones.
We pray you will never let evil have its way with us.

Deliver us to freedom's call and help those in need of you.
Shame and confuse everyone who seeks to snatch our lives.
Dishonor them and turn them away from us.
Let all who seek you find you.
Let all who seek you rejoice and be glad in you.
Let them shout continually, "great is our Lord!"
Great is our Lord, our hope and our salvation!

Praise God the Almighty. Amen

GOD'S HELP AND HEALING

But you have upheld me because of my integrity,
and set me in your presence forever.
—PSALM 41:12

Blessed Lord,

Happy is America who shelters the poor, for the Lord delivers us from trouble.
The Lord protects us, keeps us thriving, and our people happy in our lands.
The Lord shields us from those who plot our downfall and threaten our freedoms.
The Lord heals our defenders and restores their well-being.

By your grace, bring us under your sheltering wings.
Our enemies want us dead; they want to prevail in harming us.
They want us to perish and be wiped from the face of the earth.
They gather mischief, speak empty words, and tell lies to all.
They imagine the worst for us and our beloved leaders, protectors, defenders, warriors, and innocents alike.

Even our friends pretend to care, while exploiting our people.
They take our hard-earned money to enrich themselves, then turn their backs on us.
They eat from our hands, then avoid standing in solidarity with our righteous cause.
They hope in the end we will lose our powerful presence and they will rule the world.

O Lord be gracious to America and lift us up.
Show your pleasure by not letting the enemy triumph over us.
Uphold us because of our integrity, our purposeful action, and our great compassion.

Be present with us in all our moments and help us in our mission to be your hope in the world.
Let us bring your peace into all corners and capture all ears with your truths.

Blessed be the Lord, from everlasting to everlasting. Amen

BOOK II

Inspired by PSALMS 42-72

The second book of Psalms is about how <u>God goes before us.</u>

By day the Lord commands his steadfast love, and at night his song is with me, a prayer to God of my life.
—PSALM 42:8

> ### Engaging These Prayers
>
> Are you open to God leading your life? If not, why not? If so, consider how God has gone before you and made a world of difference in your life and others.
>
> Let these prayers give you wisdom to these prompts:
>
> - How does God appear in the day and the night to you?
> - Where is he leading you?
> - How do you know he's out in front?
> - How is God leading America?

We see how David pleads with the Lord to give him a clean heart and wash away his sins. No matter his situation, whether hunted, tortured, ill, heartbroken, repentant, or victorious, David shows us how to turn it all over to God and never forget to glorify him and wait on him.

As I engage these Psalms, I see how the history of evil and good plays over and over again. Different languages, different costumes, different lusts for power, but all the same human story. I see how God goes before us to prevail in all cases.

Watch how God engages with his people, as our story with him is told. See how we can express our worries, fears, cares, and concerns, and turn it all over to him. Studying God's interaction with us through prayer is the foundation of a meaningful and prosperous life. We know that God knows our hearts and minds, so he opens the door to our every thought and prayer, no matter how high or low we feel.

My prayers reflect what is going on now, and even throughout the ages, as I pray for America's cleansing, our redemption, and our salvation.

Pray with me for our beloved America.

MY SOUL PANTS

As the deer longs for flowing streams, so my soul longs for you, O God.
—PSALM 42:1

God of the Universe,

America is the deer who pants for your living water, for only you can quench our thirsting souls.
When shall we behold your face, O Lord?
We weep for our oppressed and our downtrodden.
The unknowing say, "Where is your God?"

We give you our hearts and pour out our souls to you.
We remember the joyful days when parades led to your house.
The crowds gave festivals in your name with glad tidings and thanksgiving.
Why today are we so downcast and our souls so disquieted?

Hope in God! Praise God! We know our help comes from you.

When our souls are downcast, we need only to remember you.
You prevail across our lands from mountain to valley, from shore to shore, you are there, everywhere.
Your billowing winds thunder over us, cleansing us, and refreshing us.
You command your steadfast love to care for us.

We feel at times that you have forgotten us.
When we feel oppressed, and when our enemies pierce our side, we cling to you.
When they mock, "Where is your God?" and when they disquiet our peace, we hope in you.
You are always there for us.

Hope in God! Praise God! We know our help comes from you.

You are our Rock and our Redeemer. Amen

LEAD ME TO YOUR HOLY MOUNT

O send out your light and your truth; let them lead me; let them bring me to your holy hill and to your dwelling.
—PSALM 43:3

God of Truth,

Vindicate America and defend our freedoms against ungodly and misguided politicians and their media bullhorn.
Deliver us from the deceitful who perpetrate unjust causes that harm Americans while lining their pockets.
Cure the plague and the contagion of fear that stops us in our tracks and gives us unending isolation,
For you are the God in whom America takes refuge.

Why is it possible for the power-hungry to lead unsuspecting Americans down paths of destruction?
Why do those with no wisdom, no compassion, and no good answers trap minds into believing their nonsense?
Why do the innocents get trapped and the wicked go free with their lies and criminal acts?
We need your righteous judgements God.

Vindicate the innocent and trap the wicked!
America seeks your guiding light to lead the way.
Bring America to your holy hill where truth lives in your dwelling of wisdom.
Let us approach your altar, open our eyes to see the truth, and surrender ourselves to your goodness.

Hear our pleas for your mercy and our praises of your glory.
Lift our souls and give us hope for a brighter future.
Bring us under your wings of love for your protection.
Give us your joy in living the future you destined for us.

You are our only true hope. Amen

YOU LOVE US

For not by their own sword did they win the land, nor did their own arm give them victory; but your right hand, and your arm, and the light of your countenance, for you delighted in them.
—PSALM 44:3

Father God,

America stands enveloped in the rich history of your creation.
Nations rise and fall at your hand.
Some peoples you afflicted and others you set free.
No nation wins by their own sword, or their own arm.
For it is you who brings victory for those in whom you delight.

Command victories in your name, Lord.
Let us defeat the evil enemies by your hand.
With you we push down our foes and tread on our assailants.
For we cannot trust in our own might, only in yours.
We cannot save ourselves, only you can Lord.

When we see the rise of our enemies, we feel your rejection.
We see our innocents bear the crimes of the guilty.
We see lies perpetuated upon us, guiding us into harm's way.
We see our enemies enriched by our hard-won resources.
We feel your light dim and your help diminish.

O Lord stay with us through the battles for truth and justice. Bring your righteousness and give us victory.
Do not allow our enemies to shame, disgrace, or darken us.
For we are the lighthouse for the world, fighting for life, liberty, and pursuit of happiness.
The world hopes in us, and we hope in you.

You know our hearts Lord.
Awaken and rouse yourself to our defense.
Let not one innocent succumb to vile acts or be oppressed.

Let your light shine through us.
Let your protection descend upon us.
Let us live true to you, in your full mercy and grace.

Redeem us for the sake of your steadfast love. Amen

PREPARE YOURSELF AMERICA

>...*At your right hand stands the queen in gold of Ophir.*
> —PSALM 45:9

Christ Our King,

Your bride, America, prepares herself to join you.
Her heart overflows with love for you.
She scribes joyful verses to tell of her devotion to you.
She reveres your beauty, your grace, and your blessedness.

O King secure your sword on your thigh, in your glory and majesty.
Ride victoriously for the cause of truth and defend the righteous.
Let your hand loose arrows into the hearts of your enemies.
Aim directly with your righteous anger to purge evil's cause.

Christ our King, your throne endures forever.
Your royal scepter of equity reveals your love for justice.
God has anointed you with the oils of gladness: myrrh, aloe, and cassia.
You are heartened by the wedding march from stringed instruments.

Groom, your beautiful bride stands at your side, draped in abundance.
Listen daughter, this is your King who desires your beautiful presence.
Nations will honor you and bring extravagant gifts to seek your favor.
Bow to him alone, he is your Lord deserving your undying faithfulness.

Joy and gladness lead you both into God's throne room.
You will be united as one forever and ever.
Your sons and daughters shall fill your mansions everywhere.
Your name shall be celebrated in all generations.

Praise God for this beautiful union. Amen

GOD LEADS US

Be still and know that I am God! I am exalted among the nations. I am exalted in the earth.
—PSALM 46:10

Mighty Lord,

You are America's sanctuary and our strength.
Your presence is our unwavering help in difficulty.
We shall not fear in threatening times for you are near us;
Not even when mountains shake, storms swamp cities, and winds topple homes;
Not even when people rise up in arms, and trust inside families evaporates; and
Not even when government aims to be god, driving division and tyranny everywhere.

When America peers through the darkness, we see the river of life leading to you.
Streams gurgling their gladness meander their way to your mighty fortress.
You are planted securely within America to withstand any turbulence.
Your morning dawn sends its love light to awaken hearts everywhere.
Your voice topples strongholds that threaten your peace.
You are the Lord of Hosts. You are our refuge.

Come people and see for yourselves how the Lord sends his aid.
See him disarm the power-hungry, topple wicked schemes, and bury evil dreams.
See how he ends wars everywhere, removing tyrannical dictators.
See how he destroys those seeking to overpower our will to make us slaves of the state.
Oh yes Lord, we see you are in charge.
All people will bend to your will in the end.

America hears your whispers Lord, when we listen quietly.
We quiet ourselves in your presence, so we know you are there.
You quiet our mind, give us peace, and encourage us.
You reign above every nation on earth; they all are yours.
You are the Lord of Hosts. You are our refuge.
There is no other God but you.

Our God reigns supreme. Amen

NATIONS PRAISE YOU GOD

Clap your hands, all you peoples; shout to God with loud songs of joy. For the Lord, the Most High, is awesome, a great king over all the earth.
—PSALM 47:1

Most High God, King of kings, Lord of All,

America, clap your hands in thanksgiving, and sing joyous melodies to God.
Who is more awesome than our Most High God?
He rules the world as the great benefactor and king.
He subdues insurrections and quiets rebellious mobs.
He chooses our inheritance for us, for the pride of his offspring.

God goes before us with his booming voice and the sounds of triumphant bugles.
God, your eyes roam the earth looking for saints to bear your name.
You send your angels to carry your words of salvation.
Your blood purifies our sins and you count our eternal offerings.
You make things last with hope, peace, and love.

You are our eternal hope and the source of all good things.
Praise God in the heavens for answering our cries and supplications.
Father, thank you for your healing mercies, new every morning.
Send your guardians of peace and love to provide care for the stricken.
You are needed, Lord, for your healing mercies and your peace.

Come Lord, into all the dark places to let your love-light shine.
Fulfill your promise that we may live as transformed beings.
Bring your peaceful rule into all nations and states.
America exalts your holy name and praises you for your wonderful acts, boundless grace, and unconditional love.
Sing praises to God, sing praises; sing praises to our King, sing praises.

God is the King of the all the earth. Amen

GLORIOUS STRENGTH

...His holy mountain, beautiful in elevation, is the joy of all the earth...
— PSALM 48:1,2

Great God,

How glorious you are God.
How greatly America praises you in your city on Mount Zion, home of justice and peace.
Your holy mountain, regal in its elevation, is the joy of all the earth, for America knows it seats your just and trustworthy rule.
Mount Zion presides in the center of the world with its city of our one true King.
Within its fortress you are there as a mighty defense, Almighty God.

When worldly leaders assemble near the Mount, some are astonished at its mighty presence.
Many tremble and flee in fear of you.
When they face you, they know you are God and they have no power.
They know you can scatter them to the wind, wiping their names from the chronicles of time.
In your city, the city of God, which you established forever as a mighty fortress, your rule reigns supreme.

America considers your steadfast love, O God, when we enter your temple of grace and peace.
We praise your name, knowing that you live in eternity where we may join you, and live in joy.
You are the Lord of victory and you prevail across all time and space.
Those who reach Mount Zion rejoice in you and in your gracious judgment; they know they are home at last.
Come to God's kingdom in Zion, loving persons.

Promenade along its emerald gardens.
Revel in the mighty strength of its sparkling citadels.
Camp securely behind its ramparts and unyielding fortresses.

See for yourself so you can tell your children, grandchildren, and great grandchildren timeless stories of our great God.
Tell them that he is our loving Father, forever and ever, from generation to generation and he delights in them.

Tell them how he created them.
Tell them how he pursues them.
Tell them he loves them to the ends of the earth.
Tell them he will never forsake them.
Tell them they are welcome in his kingdom on Mount Zion where they may live an eternity with him.

Come to the Lord's Mount to praise and glorify him. Amen

THE JOY OF WISDOM

*My mouth shall speak wisdom; the meditation
of my heart shall be understanding.*
—PSALM 49:3

Lord of Life,

Hear this people of America and incline your ear.
Whether rich or poor, weak or strong, high or low, this is for you.
Listen to the wisdom of the Ancient One.
Fear not in times of trouble, when the iniquities of those who trust in wealth and boast in their abundant riches invade our lives.

There is no place in heaven for earthlings who pursue wealth, and who care nothing for the fate of their brothers and sisters.
The names on their estates, their lands, and their companies may live on without them, but in death they leave it all behind.
Though the arrogant and pompous may hold riches and do well for themselves, poverty of soul brings death.
Never again will they see the light, as they descend to the company of those with the same dark fate.

Their life has no ransom, it is too costly, and no price will ever suffice to keep them from the grave.
The fate of the foolhardy and those pleased only with earthly things ends in the grave.
Death is their master and into the grave they go, where they will waste away to dust.
Torment and darkness shall be their eternal home.

Not so for those who love the Lord and submit to his Lordship.
God has ransomed their souls and receives them into his care.
They will live in his love light forever and ever.
There is no true wealth in disregarding the treasure in our souls.
Life eternal has one master who ransoms his beloved.

Trust only in him my beloved. Amen

BRING YOUR DEVOTION

Out of Zion, the perfection of beauty, God shines forth.
—PSALM 50:2

Almighty God, Merciful Father,

You are the mighty one, you are our God.
You speak to us, "America, take heed and come to judgment."
You summon all people from sea to shining sea.
From your mighty and perfect Mount Zion, your radiating glory beams forth.
Your blazing, dazzling light announces you.
Your devouring fire covers everything around you.
Your tempest winds call us to attention.
You announce it's time for judgment.

Dear Ones,
Bring me thanksgiving as your sacrifices and you honor me.
Come with me on my Way, and you shall receive my salvation eternally.
Come all my faithful ones who made covenants with me.
Come before your Righteous Judge.
Hear me as I testify about you.
Do I need you to sacrifice yourself before me?
Is there anything you can give me that I don't have?
I made all the world and everything in it is mine.
What do you think I want that you have?
What do you think I need that you can give me?
What do you have that I didn't give you?

I am your God.
Offer me your thanks.
Give me your vows and your covenants.
Make it known that you are obedient to me.
Give me your sacrifice of love, thanksgiving, and devotion.
Ask for my help in your days of trouble.
Call on me, your God.
I will give you my salvation. I shall be your God.

Listen up, you wicked ones who quote my words as if you understand my statutes.
You who act like you follow me and yet, you hate discipline and ignore everything I say.
Beware!
I see when you make friends with thieves,
When you encourage adulterers,
When you applaud abhorrent behavior, and
When you ridicule my devoted ones.

You who tell lies with every word to deceive everyone,
While pretending to be righteous,
Do you think I don't hear everything?
You who are faithful to no one,
Speaking slanderous words against anyone and everyone you choose,
Your words will turn on you.
You stand rebuked, condemned, and judged as a failure.
I will tear you to shreds and no one can help you.
Hear me for I am your Supreme God.

Stand righteous before the Lord. Amen

PARDON ME LORD AND WASH ME CLEAN

Wash me thoroughly from my iniquity; cleanse me from my sin.
—PSALM 51:2

Merciful God,

Americans must face our sins, for we have played with ideas of the evil one. We have given ourselves over to wicked acts. We have followed leaders into wrongful pathways. We have been enticed by lesser gods. We have fallen short of your glory.

Be merciful God, for you are a loving God, full of grace. In your compassion, hear our contrite heart and blot out our sins. Wash away our guilt and thoroughly cleanse us from the inside out. We see how far we have fallen away from you.

Our sins dance around us. We have only you as our escape from this dark and fallen place. Your judgment, whatever it is, is justified. We will receive your sentences, knowing how guilty we are. We are sinners through and through with no way out.

O Lord, your desire is clear. You want truth from the inside out. Purge us of our sin Lord and blank out our iniquities. Let us start fresh and new. Teach us your wise and wonderful ways that we may experience your joy and gladness in days to come.

Wipe our hearts clean and rebuild us with your righteousness. Let your joy be ours, that we may rejoice in you. Let our spirits be clean and willing to live according to your righteousness. Free us from the bondage of sin that we may be free and clear.

Set your precepts and statutes upon our souls, that we may be planted in your Word. Free our tongues to speak and teach of your wondrous ways so that we are heard everywhere. Let us give sacrifices of time, talents, and treasures to glorify you.

Receive us anew Lord, fresh and revived in your soul-cleansing love. Receive our love of you and all of your merciful ways. Let us take you with us everywhere and tell the love stories of life with you. Let our every breath glorify you.

Let us glorify and praise you in eternity, Lord. Amen

JUDGE THE DECEIVERS

*But I am like a green olive tree in the house of God. I
trust in the steadfast love of God forever and ever.*
—PSALM 52:8

Righteous Lord,

There are those who believe themselves high and mighty, walking the governing halls of America, lording over others, and mastering the art of lies with their evil tongues. See how they abuse their power, lay their deceit at the feet of others, splash them with slander, and accuse them for their own treasonous acts.

Oh yes, their lies have truth in them for they do tell all, but the names they accuse are those of the innocents they seek to destroy. They confuse, they slander, they accuse, and they pander. They boast of their mischief, toasting each other for their wins. Their treachery is deep, their intentions evil, and their lust for power is bottomless. Beware!

Open your eyes America, you are being had. Do not be deceived my beloved. Let only the truth ring in your ears. If you follow the fools, it will not end well for anyone. They want nothing but destruction. They want to be rulers without laws, enslaving the God-fearing while freeing the evildoers to tear down America's valiant history, our laws, and our very foundations.

They turn what is good upside down, applauding and encouraging what is unnatural, unhealthy, and unhelpful. They don't want happy families living peacefully in the land, earning an honest living, and worshipping God. Anything they can do to destroy this picture is their chief aim. Beware!

America, watch, listen, learn, evaluate, and validate. Trust only in those that God sends who know his truth. You will know them by the fruits of their efforts when good follows them and grows around them for those they touch. Give your allegiance only to those who make your lives healthier, happier, and more meaningful.

Live your lives deeply planted in God's Word, growing strong and healthy like an olive tree. Listen to your heart, be true to God, and keep company with the faithful. Thank God for his steadfast love and his righteous judgments.

Trust only in God! Amen

DENOUNCE THE UNGODLY

God looks down from heaven on humankind to see if there are any who are wise, who seek after God.
—PSALM 53:2

Omnipotent God,

America, you know this. It's only the fools who say that God is a figment of your imagination. No such thing as God. They want no one holding them accountable for their abominable acts and their lust for corruption. They can do no good for there is no good that lives within them.

America, God searches continuously for one good person. Is there even one good person to whom he can give his loving kindness? Are there any here in your borders, anywhere in your lands who are wise? For God gives generously and ungrudgingly to those who seek him and love him.

Has perversion and self-satisfaction overtaken everyone? Is everyone headed to the bottomless pit as they seek to feather their beds, feed their unquenchable desires, and do the unthinkable? Have they lost their minds, hearts, and souls as they cannibalize humans?

There are only two paths to choose, dear ones. God's path is above the line and leads to eternal life and goodness over the long and obedient road. The other one descends below the line to slow excruciating death of the heart, mind, and soul in company with the most corrupted spirits.

To be your own king in your own kingdom, have your own say over it all, walk the line answering only to yourself is an allusion. For you truly do not have the power within you to overcome the evil that confronts you every day. All that plagues humans requires God's help to overcome.

God, keep your search lights burning. Bring us towards your lighthouse, your perfect and beautiful citadel on your magnificent mount. Those who choose you need your help to find your lighted path. We need your comforting aid, your unconditional love, and your everlasting forgiveness.

Find us Lord and bring us home! Amen

DEFEND US PLEASE LORD

Save me, O God, by your name, and vindicate me by your might.
—PSALM 54:1

O God,

Save America by your name and free us by your strength. Justify and uphold us. Lean down and hear our prayers. Give ear to our cries. We are in desperate need of your saving grace. Our good is being shattered and our righteous ways are being reworked by wicked imaginings.

The bold, contemptuous haters have risen against us, usurping our laws to twist to their evil ends. Their ways are ruthless, without care for the hurt they cause. They seek to snub out anyone who confronts them with their wickedness. They have no use for you God or for your faithful flock.

America sees you God. You are our helper and our savior. You uphold what is good, true, and righteous. You put down evil at every turn. You end the lawlessness, suffering, and terror. You show everyone who is God. You are always victorious.

America, give all you have to God, just as he has given his all to you. Share freely your time, talents, and treasures in response to his good provision. Thank him, glorify him, and worship him, for his name is worthy and his ways are true. He delivers on his promises. He delivers you.

Thanks be to God. Amen

A FRIEND'S TREACHERY

Attend to me and answer me; I am troubled in my complaint.
—PSALM 55:2

Avenger God,

Listen to America's prayer, O God. Do not ignore our cry for help. Answer us for we are in shock at the betrayal and the treachery. Our enemies make loud threats, bring nothing but trouble, and victimize our innocents. They cause us to shake in their quest to overwhelm us.

Give us wings like an eagle so we can fly far away into the center of peace, deep in the wilderness. Let us escape our foes and go far from this wild storm of chaos. We will leave them to you Lord, to confound, confuse, and frustrate their plans for violence and conflict in our cities.

We weep at the betrayal of those who grew up with us, claimed their allegiance, acted like our friends, walked with us in the company of God, and received all our benefits. Then they turned on us, broke our laws, treated our people poorly, and turned their backs on you.

We call on you, Lord, for your love and protection. You ransom the faithful and keep them safe from the battles of their opposition. Your justice and righteousness have stood the test of time and can be counted on. You will hear us and subdue our foes.

Those who betray us win with words smooth as butter covering their hearts of war. Soothing words like lotion covering the killing daggers. They have no power with you Lord. You will send them to the pit of destruction. You will protect us and save us from their plans.

Thank you for your trustworthy saving grace! Amen

TRUST GOD ALWAYS

*Be gracious to me God, for people trample on
me; all day long foes oppress me.*
—PSALM 56:1

Faithful God,

Be gracious to America when people trample on our flag, desecrate our sidewalks, spew vile words over our honest ones, seek violence in daylight, and turn our cause upside down. Protect our warriors from murderous attempts on their lives. Reveal the depravity and mercenary tactics behind this evil to the uncertain ones tempted by their lying cause.

Put your trust in the Most High God when you are afraid, America. Praise his holy name, repeat his planted Word, seek his face, and turn to him. He will ease your fears, quiet your nerves, and give you peace. Standing on his word, no matter what is happening, you will be with him, your protector and friend.

When the ill-intended seek to spoil America's cause for freedom, when they speak lies over our shining goodness, when they twist our laws to their own ends, and when they pursue treachery against us at every turn, be there God. In every corner, in every alley, in every square, and in every home where your name is on our lips, place your hedge of protection.

O God cause the evil sent against us to boomerang against its sender, so that they retreat and leave us unscathed. You keep count of our tears, our sleepless nights, and our cries for you in your record, for nothing escapes your watchful eye. America knows you are always with us, covering us with your loving arms of protection.

America, stand firm on his rock, do not cower, and do not be afraid. Vow your allegiance to the one true God. Sacrifice with thanksgiving and praise. Recount his every Word, his every promise, and all the ways he has shown his goodness. He is your deliverer, your defender, and your eternal path. Trust in him with all your heart and follow his glorious light.

Glorify the one who is always with you. Amen

AMERICA EXALTS YOU

Be exalted, O God, above the heavens. Let your glory be over all the earth.
—PSALM 57:5

Heavenly Father,

America takes refuge in you and you alone, O God; be merciful to us. Overshadow us with your glorious wings of protection from the swirling storms. Fulfill your royal purpose in and through us, Lord.

Send your legions of angels from heaven throughout our lands to save your beloved ones. Shame anyone who tramples our peace, our people, or our future. Send forth your unswerving faithfulness that we so revere.

America exalts you, O God, above all others. We see how you send your glorious love-light over all the earth and we bow down to worship you. At your hand, those who seek to harm us get caught in their own evil traps.

You put everyone in their place according to the fruits of their heart and soul. America's heart is steadfast. We sing, praise, and worship you with joy in our hearts and love on our lips. We lift your name on high.

Praise God, the High and Holy One. Amen

COME AVENGER COME

*People will say, "Surely there is a reward for the righteous;
surely there is a God who judges on earth."*
—PSALM 58:11

Sovereign Father,

America beware of giving power to the wicked of heart. Beware of setting them in places of judgment for they distort truth, speaking lies with smooth forked tongues. They desire ultimate power over everyone, but not for good's end. They have no fairness, no mercy, and no heart.

Their work leads to suffering, loss, and violence. They rip dollars from the pockets of workers, quest after power to lord over others, and fritter away their time fabricating lies. Everyone suffers under their ill-advised plans and all progress screeches to a halt.

They were born as sinners, lying every day of their lives, going their own way from the start, and denying God to destroy all that is good. Their venom is as deadly as cobras, their ears shut to anyone's voice but their own, and their intentions birthed from dark places.

There is nothing trustworthy, true, honorable, or noble in them. Their slanderous tongues spew lies all over innocents, like true confessions of all the things they themselves have done. Yes, the lies are born from actual events, but beware, it's not those that they accuse who are guilty of treachery, it is they themselves.

America beseeches you, O God, to reveal the depth of their depravity. Break their hold on innocent unsuspecting minds. Vanish them from the public places, revoke their licenses to practice, and reveal their self-serving plans.

Let their lawless acts fall squarely on their own heads. Let their distortions of truth convict them. Let their sordid past catch up with them and expunge their power. Sweep them away from your sunlight and end their days in the sun. Dissolve their unreality so it no longer distorts America.

America rejoices in you, O God. We rejoice when you avenge all injustices. We praise your trustworthy and just ways that always prevail. We know we can rely on your righteous justice. We see who to trust by the wake of goodness they leave behind.

We give jubilant thanksgiving for the rewards on offer to those who live for you. We know you are omnipotent; all power is yours and your way is the only way. In you we rest secure. In you we find our souls' peace forevermore.

Thank you, God. Amen

DELIVER AMERICA GOD OF LOVE

*But I will sing of your might; I will sing aloud
of your steadfast love in the morning.*
—PSALM 59:16

Savior God,

Deliver America from our enemies and protect us from those who rise up against us. Deliver us from the evil work of those who seek our demise. Mercenaries buy minions to stir up trouble in the streets, promote lawlessness, attack our innocents, and our protectors. They attack because they want to destroy all that is good. They use labels of goodwill to hide their evil.

O Lord, you are the God of love and all that is good. You are our protector, our Savior, and our Advocate. Punish any persons and any nations who plot treachery against America. Fend off the prowling, howling, and growling dogs looking for their prey with mischief in their minds.

America seeks after you in our night watches, for you are our strength and our fortress. Your undying love meets us and your triumph over evil greets us in the morning. Your mirrored shield reflects prideful lies to consume evil in whole. Nothing can invade your protective legions of angels, here to save your beloved ones.

We sing praises of your mighty and powerful love. We shelter in your fortress of goodness and grace. You are our refuge, by day and by night. You are our Savior, our healer, our peacemaker, and our God. Where can we go that you are not there? Who can penetrate your protection for us? Only you can win our bodies, minds, and souls for blessed eternity.

You are our God! Amen

YOUR VICTORY OVER DEFEAT

Give victory with your right hand, and answer us, so that those whom you love may be rescued.
—PSALM 60:5

Spirit of Truth, God of Justice,

Do not reject America for the failing few or break our defenses from the misguided throngs. Do not be angry; restore your favor, O Lord. Heal the deep divisions shaking America; seal the fractures that cause us to shake. Let the threats of the government shake-down be resolved peacefully according to your laws that inform our Constitution.

Let the Word of truth have its day in the court of public opinion and let it guide America's representatives. Let all spoken lies fall like ash never to be heard. Let only truth prevail. Tune the ears of all peoples to the truth, and nothing but the truth.

Raise your flag of justice; rescue your beloved America from the precipice of collapse. Answer our fervent prayers and save us by your power. Remember your promises, delivered continuously from our very beginnings, for they are true and trustworthy. You made us rich with resources; the shining city on the hill standing for what is just and good.

All the good we have done in the world is from your hand. Keep us true to you that we may fulfill our destiny. Bring us peaceful victory in every battle we wage to protect freedom for all: battles with nation-states, battles in the governing halls, and even battles in the homes and hearts of all people.

Open any eyes that are blind to the warfare being waged for people's hearts and souls that they see what is real, true, and just. Only you God can stand with us on the side of righteousness and defend our rights and lawful actions. With your might, and only your might, can we withstand the onslaught of lying arrows aimed at our hearts to take us down and release evil powers that dominate our freedoms.

You own us God. We are yours. Give us life, liberty, and justice forevermore. Let us live out our destiny in your glorious promise of heaven, our eternal home.

Thanks be to God of truth. Amen

GOD'S PROTECTION IS SURE

From the end of the earth I call to you, when my heart is faint.
—PSALM 61:2

Welcoming God,

America cries to you. America prays to you. Listen to us Lord. Hear us when we are far, far away from you and our hearts are overwhelmed. Find us and lead us to you on your towering mount, safe from all the things that worry us.

Grant our eternity in your presence, to live close by your side and under your vaulting, sheltering protection. You have heard our confessions, our praises, and our promises to love you, our one true God. By your Word you gave us lives of freedom, and we choose you.

We bring with us those who know and love you, and you welcome them with open arms to inherit your kingdom with us. Prolong our life as a reigning nation for good, that many may live the best life for generations to come. Let your protective love watch over us.

We sing praises in your name and say vows of truth, love, justice, and peace day by day, that we may be with you to the end of time.

Praise our gracious Father. Amen

TRUST SONG FOR GOD

For God alone my soul waits in silence; from him comes my salvation.
—PSALM 62:1

Good and Gracious God,

For God alone, Americans silence our souls and wait patiently. From his hand comes everything that we need. In him alone, we live a victorious life, for he saves us for life eternal. Upon his unmovable rock we stand, protected by his fortress. He is our rock and our salvation, our mighty fortress from the whirling winds of change.

How long will the misguided assail and batter their targets? Their only plan is to bring down the protectors and the patriots. They take pleasure in falsehoods, leading others astray, winning their arguments with lies, and caring nothing for the damage they wield. They bless and curse in the same breath. Their ways lead to destruction. There is no truth in them.

For God alone, America waits in silent prayer. He gives us hope. He alone can save our future, give us steady ground, and protect our freedoms. We stand on his words of truth, solid as a rock upon which to build our dreams. Our deliverance into the brighter future and our nation's honor rests in him and him alone.

America trusts in God. We share our deepest feelings with him. He lends his ear to all of our worries, feelings, and joys. He hears our words. He sees our actions. He knows our thoughts. He is at once our refuge to regenerate and our launching pad to win another day. Our value rests in him alone, not in vain glory, in man-made estates, or in earthly riches.

There are those who believe power and prestige make them worthy. They seek it at all cost, even stooping to bribery, extortion, robbery, and treachery. They want more and more riches to build their self-image. They care nothing for their soul and its fall from grace as they strive to the highest level of their vain hopes.

Hear twice when God speaks once, America. Seek out and stand on God's truths to receive his portion of wisdom. All power belongs to God. All love flows from God. All grace is given by God. God will repay good to each one according to the good of their own doing. Set your sights on the highest good, that you may be repaid with his everlasting love.

Praise be to God, the giver of good. Amen

GOD'S COMFORTING ASSURANCE

So I have looked upon you in the sanctuary, beholding your power and glory.
—PSALM 63:2

One True God,

You are God, our God. America seeks after you in all our moments. Our souls cry for you and our bodies long for you to sustain our life in the parched and dry places where we struggle to survive. We are being strangled by the power-hungry, greedy, elitists, lawless, godless, and haters. They stand for nothing and love ripping all that is good to shreds.

For those who seek to destroy America, they will find themselves trapped in their darkness. God's sword of truth will bring to light their treasonous and evil deeds. All of their dark dreams will be ripped to shreds, left for jackals to feed upon. All the mouths of the deceivers will be bound shut and their voices silenced. All the treacherous liars will be revealed, and their devious ways exposed for all to see in your quest for justice.

There you are Lord, in your sanctuary. Behold your glory and your power! You are incorruptible and cannot be tempted by evil. Behold your goodness, your kindness, your mercy, and your grace on offer to us. Your presence beams light into the hearts of Americans who love you and seek after you. You satisfy the whole being - body, mind, and soul - with your richness.

Oh, praise the Lord America. Sing praises to his holy name. Meditate on his goodness in the night watches when sleep abandons you. He is your ever-present help and your unending aid. He covers his beloved nation in the shadow of his glorious presence. Sing for joy, cling to God, and give yourself up to him. He promises to maintain you, protect you, provide for you, and love you always.

America swears by you, Lord, for in God we trust! Amen

PRAYER FOR OUR PROTECTION

Let the righteous rejoice in the Lord and take refuge in him...
—PSALM 64:10

Protector God,

Hear us, O God, and listen to our complaints. Protect America from the threats our enemies mercilessly cast. Shield us from the plots of evil ones who are intent on our destruction. They gather in mobs and gangs lusting for dominance. Their tongues are like swords, cutting down innocents with angry words.

They ambush the unsuspecting, attacking suddenly and fearlessly. They encourage evil acts with each other, planning and setting traps in secret. They believe no-one will notice and they can never be caught. They think their plans are too perfect to be found out. They grow over-confident.

For decades, they have worked to slowly dismantle America, value by value, law by law, and thought by thought. They are cunning and driven in their malice. The unsuspecting received them, embraced them, and followed them. The power-hungry adopted their ways and played into their plans.

But God knows the human heart. He knows whose heart is cunning and bent on evil, and whose heart is good desiring the best for everyone. He sees all and he's armed to the hilt with his weapons, ready to use the sword of truth. He will expose the bad ones with their own tongues, let them drive themselves into ruin, and leave them to suffer their own treachery.

Their claims of goodness and righteousness used to cover their dark intentions have no sway with him. He will see to it that these plotters are exposed and that everyone turns their back on them.

He will stand in the gap to turn innocents away, guide them into his promises, and protect their innocence.

God, and God alone, rules the day and all people will come to proclaim his mighty acts and the amazing things he does. He will shelter America, restore our values, and secure our future. We will rejoice in the Lord and find shelter in him. We will do what is right and praise his holy name. We will be his, and he will be our God.

Thank you, Lord! Amen

BOUNTEOUS THANKSGIVING

Happy are those whom you choose and bring near to live in your courts...
—PSALM 65:4

Abundant Father,

America sings your praises from the top of our lungs. We glorify you with vows to serve you and you alone. We come to you, bend down to you, and worship you in thanksgiving. We repent our many sins, and you forgive them all, gracious Father. You answer our prayers and expunge our overwhelming guilt. How merciful you are!

You give us such joy being in your presence. The grateful ones are in your holy courts, awaiting your lavish festival of thanksgiving laid out in your magnificent temple. With your awesome deeds, you answer our prayers and set all things right according to your just ways. How generous you are!

Father, you are our savior. We hope in you. When our people travel the globe, you are there from sunrise to sunset. They climb mountain ranges that you placed across continents by your mighty power. They sail the rolling oceans with pounding waves that you quiet. They stand in awe of the wonders of your handiwork. How awesome you are!

America is in your loving care Lord. You water our lands and make them rich and fertile. Your rivers gush and gurgle with plenteous water. Your rains ensure our harvests are bountiful. Your grasslands offer lush pastures for our livestock. Your hillsides blossom with great beauty for all to behold. You carpet our valleys with grain for our flocks. How abundant you are!

Shout and sing America, for God is abundantly good! Amen

GOD'S GOODNESS TO AMERICA

All the earth worships you; they sing praises to you, sing praises to your name.
—PSALM 66:4

Glorious God,

America, raise your voice in melodies of joy and praise to God! Sing glorious tunes of his awesome name! Tell the world how wonderful he is, for you have seen his powerful deeds. Come and worship the Lord, bring your praises and your psalms. Sing alleluia, alleluia, alleluia for the Lord is good. Who is better than he? Who deserves our praises more than he does?

America, see what the Lord has done for you. His ways are miraculous and amazing to behold. Miracles abound daily from his hand. He raises people from their death bed to give them new life. He saves wee babes born pre-mature from their mother's womb and gives them new breath. He adds a century of life to the stalwart protectors of our sovereignty. Where can we look that God hasn't given life and more life?

America, raise your voice and bless his Holy Name. Your life is in his steadfast hands, protecting your every misstep from disaster. He tests your loyalty and sends you through the fire to purify you that you may be worthy of his grace. He frees your body, mind, and soul from slave chains. He carries you through fires and floods to bring you to your present abundance. What good do you have that isn't from his hand?

America, bring your honor and your promise to his holy court. Bring your sacrifices of thanksgiving and praise to place at his feet. Come tell your stories of how he listened to you, saved you, and made you new again. Confess him as your Lord for his unfailing love and submit to his perfect ways. Let him count you among his glorious tribe. What more can you want than that?

Great is our glorious God! Amen

SHINE YOUR FACE

May God be gracious to us and bless us and make his face to shine upon us, that your way may be known upon earth, your saving power among all nations.
—PSALM 67:1-2

Gracious, Blessed Father,

You shine your face upon your beloved America, Lord. You are gracious to us and you bless us. Your ways are known in the hearts of those who seek your face and learn to love you. Let your saving power be known throughout the world. Let all people praise you, O God. Let all people praise you!

Each day America is blessed to awake from the watches of the night and sit at your feet to contemplate your majestic presence in life all around us. We sense and feel your guiding hand Lord, leading your protectors and your leaders in places you appoint. Shine your light Lord and your deep abiding love wherever we carry you.

Let America be glad and sing for joy for your equitable judgments and your trustworthy guidance. Let us praise you for your abundant yield on offer to us. You have blessed us Lord, saved us for another day, and given us all that we need. May you continue to bless us that we may revere you and carry your name to the ends of the earth.

Praise God of grace and mercy. Amen

SING YOUR PRAISES

Sing to God, sing praises to his name...
—PSALM 68:4

Majestic Father,

Rise up God and scatter America's enemies. Let those who hate you run for their lives. The same for those who hate America. Blow them away like smoke and melt them like wax in the fire. Let the wicked perish in your presence God. Let the godly rejoice and be glad for you. Fill them with awe when you blaze into view riding on clouds of thunder. Fill them with joy and wonder at the awesome sight of you. Sing praises America, loud praises to your King. Rejoice in the presence of your Lord.

He is Father to the fatherless; defender of widows; matchmaker for the lonely; liberator to the persecuted; and disciplinarian to the rebellious. He is your all in all, America, for he fills every need. Just as he freed your ancestors from Egypt's cruel enslavement, he will keep you free. The earth trembles and the rains deluge the lands when he's on the march. Nothing and no one can keep him from his divine purpose to set his people free.

He settles his people in lands with bountiful harvest, abundant rain, and provisions for every need. At his command, the Holy Spirit brings truth to fill the ears of the listeners. The Almighty scatters the nations who delight in war to render them helpless. Enemies of the state and their armies flee, leaving their possessions for the godly to plunder. No one lacks for anything who sits in his presence and sings him love songs from their heart. He fills every need.

Even the majestic mountains look with envy upon Mount Zion where God has chosen his forever home. From his great Mount he comes and goes commanding heaven and earth. From his sanctuary he carries out acts of mercy and grace. He leads crowds of innocent captives to their freedom place. He receives his people and their gifts in his mansion built for human well-being. He commands acts of judgment to overrule human discord and misjudgment. He sets everything and everyone right according to his righteous truths.

America, your commander King is in charge. He is on freedom's march. He rules heaven and earth with righteous judgment. He touches human hearts and they change for the better. He casts out evil into the never lands. He offers loving kindness and freedoms like none other. No one can compare to your God. Bring your gifts of praise and thanksgiving. Praise your King, your Lord. Sing to him who rides the ancient heavens and tell everyone about his majestic power. Sing alleluia for the power and strength he has given you.

Praise be to God! Amen

GIVE US SANCTUARY

Save me, O God, for the waters have come up to my neck.
—PSALM 69:1

Savior God,

America looks to you for your saving grace. Because of our love for you, we are kicked, taunted, scorned, trapped, attacked, and mocked. Our enemies have it in for us because of you. At times, we feel like we're drowning in swamp water, standing on quicksand, turning topsy-turvy in swirling waves, ready to go down and stay down. We're hoarse from calling for you God.

All around us the liars give voice to half-truths, veiled evil intentions, and seductive thoughts that lure and entice the most innocent into their webs. We're slandered with lies that we're thieves and must pay for that which we never took. You know the truth of our life Lord. It's a wide-open book for you God. Our people look to you in hope of an innocent verdict. Don't let them be discouraged, merciful God.

When our betrayers shun us or treat us as unwanted guests, it's you they want to torture. We are the scapegoat. Though our transgressions are clear to you, you know we have stood up for you, worshipped you, and strive to be true to you. We have resisted the temptations to turn away from you that are thrown at us daily. We have stood the tests, so many Lord, so many. Don't leave us without your crown of life, gracious Father.

Don't let the swamp be our grave, or the deep dark pit be our forever home. Show your love to us God. Rid us of all mockers, naysayers, liars, attackers, and deceivers - all of the misguided serpent tongued truth-slayers Lord. Cast them down forever that they may have no more sway with human destiny. Turn the tide our way Lord. Let your Word of truth prevail in the minds of all who love you, worship you, and follow you.

Heal our wounds Lord. Bring us into your glorious sunlight and healing fresh air. Let us recover and give voice to our truths of how you save us, heal us, and love us. Let the dispirited see and be glad in you. Let the God-seekers take heart in feeling your presence. Let the poor surrender into your protective arms. Let all in heaven and earth see you Lord and praise your glorious name. Give us sanctuary in your wondrous mansions built on truth and love.

God bless America, Lord! Amen

WINGS OF GLORY

Be pleased, O God, to deliver me.
—PSALM 70:1

Our Deliverer, Our God,

Be pleased to deliver America from those seeking our demise, O God. Make haste to help us, Lord. Use your mighty powers to put those who seek to harm us into a state of confusion.

Bring dishonor and shame upon their heads, blacken their names, and blot out their power to persuade even one mind. Render them useless, helpless, and dispirited. Dishearten them, disperse them, and disaggregate them, Almighty One.

Let those in our sweet nation who seek you find you, to praise your glorious name. When we feel poorly from suffering, hasten to us, O God, for you and you alone are our help and our deliverer.

When we feel overwhelmed and in need of your loving presence, do not delay! Cover us in your loving protective wings of glory that we may be renewed, refreshed, and reinvigorated to seize another day.

In God we trust! Amen

OUR ROCK AND OUR FORTRESS

Be to me a rock of refuge, a strong fortress, to save me, for you are my rock and my fortress.
—PSALM 71:3

Sovereign Lord,

America trusts in you God and gratefully takes refuge in your loving protection. Keep us from being shamed by those clamoring for our disgrace. Lean down and incline your ear to us. In your righteousness, deliver us to our brighter future full of promise and hope. Let us stand on your rock and be our fortress, a sheltering stronghold where we are always welcome. Command our perpetual freedom from the godless with your saving words. Release us from the grasp of the unrighteous and the ruthless.

America hopes in you God. From our early beginnings, you have been our source of trust and confidence. You were there at our birth, nurtured us, and grew us into a great nation. You willed our divine mission as a nation welcoming all people to live free and flourish. You rescue us from one plot after another to weaken and enslave us. You sound the alarm when the ruling elite attempt to shift our freedoms to themselves. You send leaders to protect us from those who would sabotage our Constitution to render us helpless against those in charge.

America flourishes in you God. You sustain us through all times of war and peace, drought and floods, and scarcity and plenty. We rely on your steady hand and know you always come through. We know you are our source for love, peace, provision, and well-being. We praise your mighty and wondrous works to all. We proudly tell of your saving grace and your righteousness across centuries. We openly share our sacred memories of your miraculous deeds that tempered us, strengthened us, and made us who we are.

America gratefully and persistently glorifies and praises your holy name Lord. Amen

DESTINY OF A RIGHTEOUS NATION

Give the king your justice, O God, and your righteousness to a king's son. May he judge your people with righteousness, and your poor with justice.
—PSALM 72:1-2

Omnipotent Father,

Give America your righteous judgments and the spirit of your justice to guide our ways. May our leaders, judges, and courts rule our people, poor and rich alike, with righteousness, fairness, and equal justice. May we defend the poor, deliver aid to the needy, free the innocents, and subdue oppression. May we repay each person according to their due, in truth and justice.

Let our mountains, hills, and brooks bring prosperity to our people. May we live in peace while the sun endures, as long as the moon circles, generation to generation. May your showers water the earth, your sun grow the seeds, and your fields yield their harvest that all may flourish. May brother and sister, friend and foe lay down their weapons and silence their war-words that peace may abound.

May your freedom reign from sea to sea, from river to river, and from shore to shore, to the ends of the earth. May your enemies take their last stand and evil evaporate. May all kings, princes, and leaders give you tribute and bring their peace-offerings. May they kneel before you and their nations give you their allegiance. May your will be done throughout the earth, and throughout all time.

For you shelter the needy, poorly, widowed, lonely, helpless, orphaned, suffering, depressed, injured, violated, and oppressed. You redeem life for all and precious are they in your sight, Lord. Under your banner, America cares for them too. We shelter them and make them our cause. We act graciously towards them according to your righteousness and teach them your love Lord.

May we live long in the world. May prayer cover our every moment so that many blessings abound for us. May abundance cover our every need and sustain us through all challenges. May our beloved people blossom in our cities and countryside alike. May our name endure forever, and our fame continue as long as the sun. May all nations be blessed because of our example, for we give our full allegiance to you Lord.

Blessed be the Lord who birthed such a nation as America. Cover our warriors, strengthen their resolve, and give them tongues of truth and hearts of service. Let this nation endure in life, liberty, and happiness. Wondrous are your acts Lord, gracious are your ways, and merciful are your judgments. May your kingdom come to heaven and earth, and may all people come to know how wonderful you are.

God bless America! Amen

BOOK III

Inspired by PSALMS 73-89

The third book of Psalms is about how <u>God is all around us.</u>

The heavens are yours, the earth is also yours, the world and all that is in it — you have founded them.
—PSALM 89:11

Engaging These Prayers

As you read these prayers, reflect on how God is all around you, in your life and the life of America. What gives witness to God's omni-presence?

Let these prayers give you wisdom to these prompts:

- Where do you see God's handprints and footprints?
- What events clearly show his presence?
- What people show they are touched by God?
- How can you pray for God's presence in America?

Many of the Psalms written in Book 3 were composed for singing by Asaph, a Levite musician, appointed by King David.

The original Psalms envisioned just, righteous, and victorious rulers and kings that would usher in the eternal kingdom of peace, so the Psalms were originally dedicated to them. After the birth of Jesus, it was clear that he fulfilled the Psalms as the one true Messiah. This is why the New Testament refers often to the Psalms as prophesying Jesus.

When I began praying the Psalms, that is studying them one by one and writing my prayers as prompted, I realized how they cover the full magnitude of the human story. This makes them ever-present and meaningful for every age. I am personally amazed at how well they speak to all that is happening in America today.

As these Psalms are essentially about how God is all around us, let these prayers reveal this truth to you in your life. See how active God is. Look beyond the media stories pressing fear into lives of those around you. Look to those who inspire goodness. See how God is using them and most importantly how God is using you for his message of hope and peace.

STAY STEADFAST

Truly God is good to the upright, to those who are pure in heart.
—PSALM 73:1

Wonderful Counselor,

Truly God is good to America, to those who choose his upright ways. But many lose their footing from envying those who prosper despite their wickedness, who get a pass despite their lies, who live fat and happy with all their needs fulfilled despite ill-gotten fortunes and pay-for-play wealth accumulation.

Lord, how can it be that the wicked seem to get everything they want and live such painless lives? They are never held to account for their misdeeds, their treachery, or their lawlessness. They are pretentious and arrogant, bejeweled in pride, clothed in fashionable violence, and pampered and overfed they bulge through every silk seam.

They mock and jeer with words to kill, and bully anyone and everyone to get their own way. They're filled with vile hot air that they spew on everyone to disturb the peace. How people can listen to them and let themselves be swayed to their wayward thinking is unbelievable. How they can respond like puppies lapping up their every lie is unthinkable.

So how is it God that the wicked get by with everything and the upright are harassed and sentenced? How can they live high on the hog while the righteous barely scrape by? Where is the justice in the good ones having to suffer the crimes of the evil ones? Where is your righteous justice, O Lord?

Hear my answer dear one. I am your God. Come, for you are precious to me. Let me bring you to your senses and keep you from betraying me. I will open your eyes to see as I see. I will lead you into my sanctuary where all truth is revealed and where you can reach understanding. I will let you see the whole picture, for you see so little.

The wicked are on the slippery road to destruction. They will swerve into the ditch of their delusions. In the dark night's blind curve, they will crash into their worst nightmare. In an instant, a blink of an eye, they will experience disaster. The fire will consume them in full and their memory will dissipate forever. Their fate is sealed.

Here now, America, take my hand. I will guide you in your stubbornness and ignorance, for I know while you question me, you have always loved me. I know that you have suffered much, and still I am all you want. I know you want to live with me in my heavenly kingdom. You have been faithful to me and I will be always be faithful to you.

O God, America is home in you. Glorious is your sanctuary. Amen

HELP FOR A HUMILIATED NATION

*Direct your steps to the perpetual ruins; the enemy
has destroyed everything in the sanctuary.*
—PSALM 74:3

Please God,

Why have you become distant from us? Why have you let American cities that were once beacons of prosperity devolve into wastelands of human tragedy? People without homes take up residence on the promenades, desecrate the sidewalks, leave their drug-filled trash wherever they loiter, and panhandle for their next bite. The cities, once the prize of America, are now trash heaps of human discard, the result of human discord.

Is it because the norm became to remove your teachings from the planet? Is it because people let the serpent-tongued lies drown out your laws of good living from the hearts of mankind? Is it because your foes subdue your people and destroy your sacred places in the name of equity? Is it because your people became so prosperous under your blessings, they grew pompous and self-centered, and forgot it was all because of you?

There are infinite reasons to let your cities and your people fall into the shame and disgrace of their own making. They are due your wrath for turning their backs on you and driving others to do the same. And yet, we your people still need you Lord. You showed us your love when you parted the seas, cut off Leviathan's head, and dried up flowing rivers to let us pass into your promised land. You sustained the generations on your love and your provision to show us you are our God.

Reveal your face again Lord and extend your hand. Help your people rebuild the temple within. Show them how to stem the tide of human "Devil-ution." Do not deliver your beloved doves to the wild jackals who feed on bloody destruction. Empower your light-workers to cast miracles into this mess, to achieve historic human cleanup like none have ever seen, to free minds, hearts, and souls to find your song within, and to bring about the renovation and restoration of your kingdom on earth.

By your power let us win to praise you for evermore. Amen

THE WONDER OF GOD

...I will rejoice forever; I will sing praises to the God of Jacob.
— PSALM 75:9

Gracious Lord,

America gives our grateful praises and thanks to you for your everlasting love and provision. You answer our prayers according to your will. You cover us with your blessings of the heart. You sustain us with your holy actions. You give us prosperity throughout the generations. You save us from ourselves and from our foes. You are our all in all.

You ask three things of us supreme Lord: that we fear you by giving allegiance to your holy name; that we stamp your love-laws upon our hearts to act in reverence to them; and that we humble ourselves, and not exalt ourselves above those on our right and left, for we are all equal in your sight. When we follow your simple commands, you grow the joy of life within us.

You judge with equity, righteous One, at the times that you appoint. Let America be patient and stand firm on this Lord, for you know the perfect timing for all to be revealed. You rebuke the wicked, silence the insolent, and uphold the righteous. You steady a tottering America on its capital pillars that your justice may reign supreme. You set all things right.

No one from the east, west, north, or south can lift up America. Only by your hand is judgment executed. You put down one and lift up another according to each one's due. In your hand is the cup of wrath that you force the wicked to drink to its dregs, ending their reign of terror. You leave the righteous free to sing your praises and rejoice in you forever.

Sing praises to God, America, for he is your all in all. Amen

SOVEREIGN JUDGE

*There he broke the flashing arrows, the shield,
the sword, and the weapons of war.*
—PSALM 76:2

Supreme Lord,

You are well known across America, even a household name. Your name stands supreme in the hearts and homes of those who love you. Even in the haunts of those who deny you, you are known. Nowhere can we go that your name isn't there, above all others. You are our supreme Lord and king!

In your dwelling place in Zion, you made a bonfire of all guns, machetes, bombs, drones, tanks, and instruments of war. Everything gone in a flash, wiped out of the hands of militants and warmongers. War no more. Only peace may reign in your kingdom. Only goodness and kindness can rule the day!

So glorious are you God, more majestic than the mountains of evermore. You shine brighter than any plunder gathered in the spoils of war. You withdraw the loot of war-lust demons and leave them impotent. You rebuke and stun war hungry ingrates in their tracks. You destroy their swagger and threats in an instant. They cannot stand against you.

You are a God of vengeance! Who can survive before you when your anger is roused? From heaven your judgment thunders against all oppressors, knocking them to their knees in breathless fear. You rise, standing taller than the tallest peak, to save your people from unspeakable fate. You fire your anger as a scourge to eliminate the dregs of humanity.

God, you wrap demons' wrath like a garland of glory around your waist. Their smoldering rage becomes the prize of war. You create order from chaos, stop evil in its tracks, and pour war-mongers' wild temper upon their own heads. You hold everyone to account. No matter their standing on earth, no one gets by with their sins against humanity.

All praise and glory to you, supreme Lord! Amen

REMEMBER HIS GOODNESS

*You are the God who works wonders; you have
displayed your might among the peoples.*
—PSALM 77:14

Wondrous Lord,

America's soul is weary Lord. We cry out in our grief. We wail loudly that you might hear us. We search for you in the deep dark night. We lift our hands to your heavens, praying for your consolation. No one else can comfort us. When we think of you, we ache to see your peaceful face. We yearn to feel your reassuring presence. We long for your restoration.

Our worries keep sleep at bay. We remember fondly the times when nights are filled with joyful dreams. We ponder our circumstances wondering why things are so different. Have you left us Lord? Rejected us? Spurned us? Turned your back on us? Forgotten us? Is your compassion for us no more? Or, is this what our grief does? Increase our distance from you?

For our memories of your wonders and deeds are so full and so rich. We remember no time when you were not there by our side. You created us, pursued us, taught us, saved us, and loved us. From our formation, you set your commands within our laws to bring order from chaos. You set all things in place to grow and nurture us. You walked beside us, guarding and protecting us, day by day.

You paint water-color skies to greet our mornings. You raise the magnificent sun to light our days. You set moon and stars over the night watches to guard our dreams. You bring sheer joy in babies' laughter to grow our family. You paint our world beautiful. With footprints unseen, you lead us and give us entry to your kingdom. Where can we go that you are not there, God? Even in our grief.

Thank you, God, for helping us to remember you, even in our troubles. Amen

WIN OUR SOULS AGAIN

*In the daytime he led them with a cloud, and
all night long with a fiery light.*
—PSALM 78:14

Most High God,

America is like Israel. You have given us every blessing. You birthed our forefathers who gave us life, liberty, and pursuit of happiness. We have enjoyed great prosperity and power at your hand. Our people have grown up strong, healthy, and hopeful in your sunlight. When everyone was on top of the world, powerful leaders in their appointed places, and people relishing their good fortunes, they forgot about you. They chose to be their own gods; do things their own way; and deny your power and provision.

America has not kept our covenant with you, even though you have acted in wondrous ways. Pompous Americans have forgotten what you have done, they speak against you, and they do not trust you - their creator and provider. They have not fulfilled their covenant to you. America has legs of clay on sinking sand. Denying your wisdom and guidance over decades, we have chosen leaders who pushed us over the cliff.

Yet among those who are stiff-necked, smug, belligerent, and misguided are those who are true to you Lord. For the sake of all the generations who have worshiped you and fought the good fight with you Lord, turn your anger and your wrath away from your faithful community and point it to those who don't know your name or the covenant you have always honored.

Give freedom and leadership to your nation Lord, that we may live in your good graces and join you in your work of redemption for this fallen race. Have mercy Lord and move your mighty hand across this land to touch the hearts of people for good; give us a future of hope and benevolence. O Lord, move the mountains of deception and ignorance, move the winds of injustice, and lead this fight with us for the soul of America.

Come Lord come, we pray. Amen

HAVE MERCY ON AMERICA

Help us, O God of our salvation, for the glory of your name; deliver us, and forgive our sins, for your name's sake.
—PSALM 79:9

Lord Our God and Our Salvation,

People that are not your people are invading America. For decades, they have come into our porous borders claiming the lie of persecution, yet their desire to persecute and change America sits deep in their hearts. They desire to take over America and rule with power and privilege, while persecuting all who do not give allegiance to their ideology or promote their godlessness.

They have no desire to be American, for they proclaim evil against America. They don't respect our history, our laws, or our people. They have no desire to assimilate within America, only to violate us, change us, rule against us, and destroy us. They are moving quickly into our halls of government to pursue their take-over.

These invaders have turned their face against you and believe a different gospel - a gospel of hate, violence, and oppression – claiming they do this in your name. Blasphemy! Your gospel is a gospel of love and freedom, kindness and goodness. Men and women believe these lies because they are lured and deceived into thinking in perverse ways.

Their ways lead only to disaster in the end. They are disastrous for America. How can this happen Lord? How can people use your glorious name in perverse ways? How can those who have grown up in America welcome such perversion? How can they vote them into positions of power to change our very essence?

Oh Lord, remember your promises that are trustworthy and true. Remember your plan to prosper and not to harm America. Remember your mighty acts of redemption. Your flock is unable to fight the principalities of evil without your hand, your heart, your good, and your power. Your flock stands aghast at what is happening in America, watching the cycle of evil rear its ugly heads.

America knows you have always been there for us, and always will be. Strengthen our leaders and our people fighting against the principalities of darkness that invade the very hearts of men and women. Don't withhold your hand from us; let us be victorious. For your way is the only way to peace, prosperity, and freedom on offer to every soul.

Wake up America; let your slumber be at end. Do not be deceived by anyone. Seek the truth, for if you don't, you will lose all that is precious to you. Fight for the truth. Fight for what is right. Test everything to see if it truly leads to life abundant. Follow only leaders set in place by God who help our people grow and thrive.

God, awaken America to your ways and your truths and bring victory forevermore. Amen

RESTORE AMERICA

Give ear, O Shepherd of Israel...Stir up your might, and come to save us!
— PSALM 80:1,2

Our Shepherd, Our Lord,

Let your face shine upon America that we may be saved. Display your radiant glory. Awaken your mighty power. Come and rescue us. Turn us to face you so we may see you clearly and hear you truly. O God of heaven's armies place a shield around us that no lie can penetrate.

Your adversary is encroaching our hallways in government, businesses, schools, and homes. He is encroaching our innocents' minds, to pervert them, even our most precious little children. O Lord don't let him not have his way with us. O God of heaven's armies protect our precious ones that they may remain untarnished.

Turn us again to yourself. Let your face shine again on us. Only then will we be saved. O Lord, how long will you be angry with us? You have fed us with sorrows and buckets of tears. Your adversary scoffs at us, penetrating our defenses to win us away from you and corrupt us. O God of heaven's armies place a hedge around us to resist his cunning ways.

You brought a vine of your family here to plant in America. You cleared the ground for it; it took deep root and filled the land. It covered the mountains, ran its network around mighty oaks, sent its roots to the seas, and its shoots to the rivers. Why then have you let your adversary penetrate our walls and steal our precious fruit? O God of heaven's armies guard your sweetest vine.

Turn again to us now. Peer down from your mount and regard our current state, the living vine of your family that you planted here. Don't let evil burn it with fire, kill the innocents, and tear it down. Rebuke the adversary Lord. Strengthen the vine that you love, the one of your choice. Bring us back to you, never to turn away again that we may praise you all of our days! O God of heaven's armies restore us.

Bring us home to you, O God of heaven's armies. Amen

A STUBBORN AMERICA

O that my people would listen to me, that Israel would walk in my ways!
— PSALM 81:13

Lord God, Our Mighty King,

Great is your name for all time. Wondrous are your acts of redemption. Boundless is your love for your created people. Tender is your mercy. Bottomless are your saving ways. Majestic are you our God. Glorious is your grace. Supreme are your judgments. Superior are you, King of glory.

Yet America houses self-absorbed people with stubborn hearts, choosing destructive counsel. See where we lead ourselves without your guiding hand. We become slaves to unnatural ideas, overpowered by evil ones with vastly destructive schemes. Our people have become downtrodden, disenchanted, rebellious, and violent. The world around us unravels.

In times like these America's faithful can count on you. You relieve our shoulders of burdens, and free our hands from chains. You release our minds and our souls from darkness. You rescue us from distress and heal our broken hearts. You are the Lord our God who brought us out of lost lands, where people believed they were divine rulers of all things, and where life was overtaken by what the flesh desires.

You bring us into your life where you rule and yet give us the freedom to choose your way if we want. You fill our mouths with all we need of the very best. We need your rescuing arms, more than ever, Lord. Overthrow the principalities of evil. Move through America in a moment and turn our hearts towards honor, goodness, and righteousness. Send your legions of angels to save us Lord and overwhelm all evil.

Thank you for your everlasting kindness and steadfast love. Amen

RULE THE DAY

Rise up, O God, judge the earth, for all nations belong to you!
—PSALM 82:8

Divine Majesty, Supreme Ruler, Prince of Peace,

Even in America, there are men and women with power who think that they are god, yet they judge innocents unjustly, and show partiality to the wicked. The little gods have no knowledge or understanding. They walk around in darkness. They speak only lies and deceive everyone.

God, you are the divine judge and ruler of the universe. Your judgment gives justice to the weak and the orphan. You maintain the rights of the lowly and the destitute. You rescue the weak and the needy. You deliver everyone from the hand of the wicked. Your way is the only just way.

The foundations of the earth are shaken, and the earth spins off its moral compass. The core truths of life - your truths, your powers, and your love - are being trampled on. Chaos rules the day, godlessness is taking over, seizing all innocents in its path and converting them, killing them, or oppressing them.

Arise true judge of all the earth. Send the little gods to their early graves and make them dust under your feet. Free your nations from the squanderers, evil doers, and ideologues bent on disastrous ways. Raise your hand and all will be right again. Speak the Word, Lord, speak the Word, and let freedom, justice, and peace rule the day.

All praise and glory to our Sovereign Lord. Amen

DECIMATE EVIL

O my God, make them like whirling dust, like chaff before the wind...Let them be put to shame and disgraced forever.
—PSALM 83:13,17

Our Most High God Over All the Earth,

Let America hear from you Lord. Do not keep silent, hold your peace, or be still. Our enemies are scheming, planning, and killing. Anyone who knows the truth of the treacherous deeds against us is in peril. Many protectors of truth and freedom have been murdered. Even your healers are being silenced.

Innocents are dying of the invisible enemy unleashed upon the world and the crime is being silenced. Your adversary has lured puppets into his crafty plans, and they consult together against those you love and protect. They are intent on obliterating the little people, to leave only the elites who deserve to have it all.

Take on these sick leaders who are your enemies and make them dung for the ground. Make them whirling dust like the chaff of wheat, dispersed to every corner of the earth. Use your fire and flame to consume them. Pursue them with your tempest and decimate them with your hurricane.

Shame evil doers in high places and disrupt their evil plans. Make them perish in disgrace, bent and beaten. Even America's protectors and warriors need your protection, Lord, for they are fighting the battle of the ages - good against evil. Extend your arm overall and call heaven's armies for the war has escalated and only you can win this with us at your side.

Bring peace to America and our faithful.

For you alone are the Lord, the Most High over all the earth. Amen

JOYOUS WORSHIP

For a day in your courts is better than a thousand elsewhere...
—PSALM 84:10

Glorious Father,

You are America's Lord, America's God, and America's strength. There is no place we would rather be than in your courts - your lovely dwelling place. Just thinking of being with you makes our hearts leap with joy and peace, and love descends to the roots of our beings.

Happy are we to be in your dwelling place, our only true home, where you reign supreme with justice, righteousness, love, and security. Happy are we who trust in you and gain our strength from you. Ever singing your praises brings great celebration for there is no end to the stories of your saving grace in the lives of your people who love and worship you.

Happiness settles in our lands and in the hearts of our people like the fresh dew of morning. Even our sparrows and swallows sing to your glory from their nests at your altar. We are crowned in your loving kindness and your joy, for great is your faithfulness. God, you are our sun and our shield. We pray to remain with you for all eternity.

America, lift your voices and renew your hearts, for your Lord and Savior is at hand. Come and worship him to bring joy to your hearts.

Thank you, Lord. You are greatly loved. Amen

RESTORE YOUR FAVOR

Steadfast love and faithfulness will meet. Righteousness and peace will kiss each other. Faithfulness will spring up from the ground, and righteousness will look down from the sky.
—PSALM 85:10

Righteous Lord,

You look upon America with favor and forgive all our iniquities. When we go astray, you pull us back within your reach to remind us of your great and faithful love. You seat us in your company and recount the stories of your saving grace for us.

You restore us Lord and release the indignation you have for our misguided and rebellious ways. You put away your hot anger, pardon our sins, and pour your consuming love upon us in memory of the hope you created so long ago.

You remind us of your ways that shed light upon your glorious path. You recount the stories of old when you led us out of condemnation and slavery to release us from our oppressors and grant us your salvation.

You set us aright, cleanse our souls of our sins and failings, and renew our minds. You speak peace to us and talk about your plans to prosper us, to give us hope and a bright future. You reveal that your mercy is at hand for our faithfulness in turning back to you.

Lord, we can sit at your feet for hours and relish in your goodness and your faithfulness. We put you on high Lord and glorify your name. We praise you as our one true and righteous God, our Creator, our Savior, and our Redeemer. We are fulfilled in you. May everyone receive God's steadfast love, faithfulness, righteousness, and peace.

Glory to God in the heavens and on earth! Amen

MOST WONDERFUL

Teach me your way O Lord that I may walk in your truth...
—PSALM 86:11

Heavenly Father, Merciful and Gracious God,

Listen to America's cries. We seek your mercy and grace to come and be present in our times of trouble. Protect and preserve us Lord for we are fully devoted to you.

When we call upon you, we know you will incline your ear and listen to our pleas for justice and righteousness. For you are Sovereign, full of steadfast love and slow to anger.

All the nations will see the folly of worshiping manmade gods, turn to you, and bow down before you. You are the only miracle worker with works too magnificent to contemplate.

In our times of poverty and need, when we languish and suffer, we can depend on you, and you alone, for you are great and do wondrous things. Your strength, patience, and wisdom are unparalleled.

You are the purveyor of all truth and the Creator of all good. You teach the way of truth and life to all who come to you, that life may be beautiful.

We seek your teachings that we may honor and glorify you in and through our lives. Give us undivided hearts, O Lord. We give thanks to you with our whole beings and glorify you.

You redeem and deliver us from death's valley where our enemies lay in wait to attack us and where death looms heavy. You overcame death that you might call us home.

Though we sin, when we repent, we find you. For you are merciful and gracious, slow to anger, and abounding in steadfast love.

Praise God. Great is your faithfulness. Amen

JOY OF LIVING WITH GOD

Glorious things are spoken of you, O city of God.
—PSALM 87:3

Most High God,

You established Zion, your city, the universal city of all nations that all may be born into it. You established this city where you welcome all and you rule all in justice, righteousness, and love.

Let those from America and from all nations rise to your great city on the mount. May all people be privileged to be born in your city under your wings. Your gates are opened wide to all who come in under your shelter.

Love enfolds and surrounds your people in Zion, and they exclaim the wonder of your magnificent name. People dance and sing to your glory with great and exuberant joy.

O Lord, America cries for the day when we are free from sin, strife, violence, and suffering. We praise your holy name without ceasing for we know you are our one true God. We live in hope of a bright future where your sovereign reign rules all.

Lord, bless America and let us be a blessed city like your Zion. Let our rulers govern with your hand. Let corruption be a thing of the past. Let our people sing with joy and praise your name forever and ever.

Glorious is our Most High God. Amen

IF WE ARE NO MORE

Let my prayer come before you; incline your ear to my cry.
—PSALM 88:2

God of the People, Sovereign Lord and Master,

America cries out to you Lord. Incline your ear to us and hear our pleas. Too many of our innocents are trapped in the pit of lies with no hope. We are forsaken like the dead, like those slain and lying in the grave, cut off from your memory and your helping hand.

We are in the regions dark and deep, led there by lying leaders, with wrath growing all around us and pulling us in two. We are faced with two fates, one leading to your glorious Zion and one leading to the valley of death. We call on you to work wonders for us.

Can we praise you from the grave? Can we declare our allegiance to you if we are no more? Can you declare your steadfast love to us if we are ashes? Can you tell of your awesome faithfulness if we are dust? Can we remember and praise you all day long if we are a lost memory?

We seek your face Lord, your mighty hand, and your saving grace to rescue us. In rags, we kneel and pray from dawn to dusk, asking for your forgiveness. Do not cut us off, Lord, or hide your face from us. Do not send treasonous, treacherous leaders to lead us to no tomorrows. Do not call the darkness to close in on us Lord.

Remember your faithful America, though we are sinners, we call on you and seek your will that we may find your day of forever peace where life, liberty, and pursuit of happiness win each day. We stand on your promise of life with hope and a future of glorious tomorrows.

Come Lord come. Amen

GOD'S FOREVER PROMISE

*I declare that your steadfast love is established forever;
your faithfulness is as firm as the heavens.*
—PSALM 89:2

Creator God, Steadfast and True,

America sings of your steadfast forever love. We proclaim your undying faithfulness benefiting us for generations. When you created America, you established your covenant with us to continually bless our descendants in all our yesterdays, todays, and tomorrows. We praise you and glorify your name.

You are the Holy One among all the heavenly beings. Even the council of the holy ones lifts your name on high. There is none other as great, as awesome, and as mighty as you, Lord. You rule all of heaven and earth with unparalleled righteousness and justice. The heaven is yours, the earth is yours, the world and all that is in it, you created it all.

Who can surpass you, Lord? Who can break your covenants that you made with your people? What happens in the skies, on the seas, or on land that is not from your hand? Who is more awesome than you? Who is mightier than you? Who else can America turn to in full trust knowing we will be heard?

Righteousness and justice are the foundation of your rule, Lord, and steadfast love and faithfulness go before you. Happy is America when we walk in the light of your countenance, when you make your face to shine upon us, when you pour light into the darkness to reveal our path. Happy are we when we are free to exalt your name as often as we want.

We pray Lord you do not take your hand away or leave us to suffer. Let us pay penance for our sins that you might temper us, but do not leave us in despair Lord and forget those who love you. Our need for you arises from every cell in our bodies, every wish in our hearts, and every thought in our minds. O great healer make us whole in your image.

We pray for your everlasting healing justice that we may remain in your house forever. Forgive our iniquities, remove our transgressions, cleanse our souls, heal us from the inside out, and bring us home to Zion, Lord, for great is your faithfulness. Remember your covenant with us and let America stand as one nation under God now and forever.

Bless you, our forever Lord. Amen

BOOK IV

Inspired by PSALMS 90-106

The fourth book of Psalms is about how <u>God is above us.</u>

He has established this world; it shall never be moved; your throne is established from old; you are from everlasting.
—PSALM 93:2

Engaging These Prayers

Consider God in all his majesty and who you are in relation to him. Consider the eternal nature of his words, his works, and his wisdom.

Let these prayers give you wisdom to these prompts:

- How does God demonstrate his supremacy?
- How do you feel in relation to God?
- How does God inspire goodness in you?
- How can you pray for God to be above America?

God is above us. In fact, God is above everything. God is the creator of everything. He is the author of all good. That is really good news. He has a plan for redemption – that is the great story that the Bible tells us. That is the great good news. In fact, that is the story that Jesus fulfilled. He made it his mission to carry out God's plan for redemption for all people, and he fulfilled his mission.

If God is above us and in charge of everything, then why is there so much evil in the world? This is the biggest question every person has to grapple with in understanding God's plan. The answer speaks to what faith is all about. If God commanded us to believe a certain way and act a certain way, he would have taken away our free will. Forcing us to love him is contrary to his nature. We must choose our relationship with God.

One of our greatest gifts from God is our free will, and it's at the heart of what makes America great. It is the basis for our Declaration of Independence - life, liberty, and pursuit of happiness. Each person has to come to know God on his/her own terms. Each person has to see and experience what it is like to live without him and what it is like to live with him.

God gives his love freely. You have to open yourself to accept his love. He takes your life in his loving hands when you freely give it to him. Your greatest adventure in life is learning to trust in him, give yourself over to him, and put him above yourself. God can do so much more in and through your life than you can even imagine! It's up to you.

MASTERFUL GOD

...From everlasting to everlasting, you are God.
—PSALM 90:2

Everlasting Majestic Father,

You are America's God from everlasting to everlasting.

By your hand, we possess great talents to master for bringing about your good. You have created a masterpiece in each one of us. We are your great master work.

Your work is manifest in and through us and your glorious power through our children. You give us purpose and meaning to make the world a better place where peace and justice rule.

May your favor be upon us that we grow up our children as great masters of beauty, peace, justice, and prosperity to benefit the world through all generations.

May we partner with you Lord that we may come to know your wise ways and maximize our gifts that you bestowed upon us. May we recognize the source of all power for love and goodness.

Move your powerful hand across the nations Lord, protecting and defending your good people and leading them to victory on all fronts.

Anything humans have made that results in harm of any kind to anyone, bend for good by your graceful hands. Make all things new by your saving grace. Have the last say Lord.

For you are our God, from everlasting to everlasting. Alleluia! Amen.

BLESSED ASSURANCE

Those who love me, I will deliver; I will protect those who know my name.
—PSALM 91:14

Most High God, Mighty Savior and Protector,

You are America's God in whom we trust.

You provide us shelter when we abide in your shadow, as followers who love you, adore you, and hold fast to you.

You cover us with your wings, as an eagle covers its young, that we may find shelter in you.

You shield and protect us with your faithfulness from the slings of enemy arrows, terrors of the night, and evil lurking by day.

You punish the wicked for their harmful deeds, while protecting your beloved people who have made you their dwelling place.

You command your angels to come to our aid, to guard us from those who want to poison us with their venom.

You love us with such great care Lord, meeting our needs and protecting us from the deadly schemes of your adversaries.

You have set before us laws that free us for happy lives, without overreach of a government that steals our future to make us their slaves.

Protect your beloved America in this way Lord and deliver us to the future you have planned for us, one filled with life, liberty, and pursuit of happiness.

Oh Lord Most High - we are yours. Let us live in your dwelling now and forevermore.

You created us and in you we live and have our being. Amen

GREAT THANKFULNESS

It is good to give thanks to the Lord, to sing praises to your name, O Most High; to declare your steadfast love in the morning and your faithfulness by night.
—PSALM 92:1-2

Sovereign Lord,

You are the Most High God.

America praises you and makes music in your name. We proclaim our love for you in the morning and our faithfulness to you at night.

By your deeds, you satisfy our needs. We joyfully sing praises to you for all that your hands have given us. We see your glorious works on display from dawn to dusk. We harken to your thoughts that give Word to all of creation. We know your wondrous way.

Those who do not see you are blind to the blessings of living life with you. Those who shut you off, shut off the better parts of themselves. Those who do not seek to know and understand you live half a life pursuing their limitless desires, never to be fulfilled.

Your enemies are our enemies. Our enemies are your enemies. Surely you will scatter the evildoers and defeat the adversary's pawns. The wicked ones will perish in the darkest night. No one can withstand the wrath you display when your people are harmed in any way.

You show the righteous how to flourish in their lives. You provide everything that is fresh, green, and alive from your hand to the faithful. You give life everlasting to those deeply planted in you.

You are America's rock and our salvation. Amen

MAJESTIC RULER

Your decrees are very sure; holiness befits your house, O Lord, forevermore.
—PSALM 93:5

Lord God, King of Kings,

You are enthroned in majesty, robed in strength.

You are from days of old, from everlasting to everlasting.

You created the world and all that is in it.

You tamed the roaring waters and raised the land.

You are more awesome than rolling waves in thunderous seas.

You are more amazing than the sparkling stars flung across the blackness.

You are more lofty than the brilliant sun kissing the regal mountain tops.

Nothing compares to your majesty, Lord.

America needs only to hear and do your words, your holy, holy words.

Help us bring heaven on earth Lord.

Help us bring moral, ethical leadership to rule for our people, for in you we trust to bring about good for all.

Put down all lies, corruption, and deceit by your righteous decrees.

Open people's eyes to your truth Lord.

Touch the soul of each and every elected leader that they might lead with your wisdom and your heart.

America trusts in you and you alone, Holy Father.

Bring your majestic rule to oversee us.

Thank you, Father! Amen

AVENGER GOD

For the Lord will not forsake his people; he will not abandon his heritage.
—PSALM 94:14

O God of Vengeance,

You know all and you see all.
Rise up, shine forth, and judge the earth.
America needs you Lord. Avenge us from the wicked.
We are hollow vessels without your lovingkindness.

How long will they be exalted?
How long will they pour out their arrogant words?
How long will they boast of their treacherous victories?
How long will they get away with murdering the innocents?

How long will they get away with attacking the lost and forlorn?
How long will they gather treasures from the unsuspecting?
How long will they call you fiction in the minds of the dullards?
How long will they continue their charade?

Lord, you hear all - did you not create the ear?
You see all - did you not create the eye?
You know our thoughts - did you not create the mind?
You teach all knowledge - did you not create all that is real?

Come now Lord and teach your beloved America the wisdom of the ages, and the laws of good living.
Give us respite from days of trouble until all wickedness is captured and caged.
Return your righteousness and justice to the upright in heart.
Rise up against the wicked and stand up for us against evil.

Let us see your hand in the world.
Let us praise your name and cast our cares to the wind.
Let us enjoy the day and all the people in it.
Let us live in your everlasting peace.

Come, our God the great avenger, come. Amen

OBEDIENT WORSHIP

Let us come into his presence with thanksgiving...
—PSALM 95:2

God of All Blessing, Shepherd of Peace,

Let America remember your steadfast love and your faithfulness, for you are God above gods and King above kings.

Let us sing joyful songs of praise and thanksgiving.

You hold the depths of the earth and the heights of the mountains in your hands.

You formed the seas and the dry lands by your Word.

You called the world into being, all its creatures and your people, Lord.

You clothed us, fed us, and gave us a calling to love and serve you and your people.

You deserve our stalwart loyalty, given on bended knee with praise and thanksgiving.

O Lord and Master, accept our love and let us come into your kingdom, purified by your fires, and cleansed by your blood.

Free us from the schemes of the evil one who has turned the hearts of weak men and women against you and your people.

Open the eyes of all to see the truth of corruption in America, especially in the unworthy elected in whom we put our power.

Open our eyes, hearts, and minds to choose our best path forward at the crossroads of renewed hope or death's dark call.

CYNTHIA J STEWART

Thank you for hearing our fervent prayers.

In you and you alone Lord, America lives free.

Praise be to God, the One we love. Amen

GOD RIGHTEOUS JUDGMENT

Sing to the Lord, bless his name; tell of his salvation from day to day.
—PSALM 96:2

Supreme Lord, Ruler of All People and All Nations,

America sings a new song in your name.

We bless you and submit to your just rule.

We desire your victory that all nations unite in your name.

Across millennia, you have shown your steadfast love, by giving the world and its people all they need to grow and thrive.

Even the heavens, moon, stars, oceans, and all of nature itself declare your splendor and your magnificence.

You are everywhere all the time, healing illness and brokenness through your saving grace.

Great is your name Lord. Great are you!

May we honor your majestic name in the strength and beauty of your sanctuary.

Thank you, Lord God, for all the ways you manifest your goodness and deliver your salvation.

Thank you, Lord God, for all the ways you prove your great love for your people.

Thank you for judging the world with righteousness and all the people with your truth.

O Lord, thank you for giving America back to our people and giving us a brilliant future for our people to live out our days in freedom, peace, and prosperity.

May we worship you in holy splendor. May we praise and glorify your name forevermore.

God of goodness and strength, we love you. Amen

OUR GOD REIGNS

The heavens proclaim his righteousness; and all the peoples behold his glory.
—PSALM 97:6

Glorious King of All Heaven and Earth,

You reign over all with goodness, righteousness, and justice. Let us be glad and sing praises to your name.

Is there anything else America can do but rejoice at the sound of your name? All of your created rejoice!

The coastlands roar aloud with the crashing waves in honor of you Lord. The stalwart mountains rise to meet in your glory.

Your fiery anger clears all evil out of your path as you cleanse the lands and your peoples' hearts.

Your lightening dashes forth, lighting the darkness, and revealing all evil that you may end it once and for all.

Those who won't say your name and who rely on their little gods evaporate before you.

The heavens proclaim your righteousness, revealing your glorious expansive love.

The city of God, Zion, and all places where your beloved people dwell, rejoice at your power and glory.

You are the Most High God, exalted above all little gods, kings, magistrates, and the self-proclaimed high and mighty.

Your faithful and righteous believers find their home in you, and respite from the wicked.

CYNTHIA J STEWART

Thank you, Lord, for ending the evil plans of your adversaries and bringing sheer joy to the upright and good.

America rejoices in you Lord and gives thanks to you for purging evil to let us live our days in your mercy and grace.

Rejoice in the Lord and praise his holy name. Rejoice! Amen

JUDGE OF TRUTH

O sing to the Lord a new song, for he has done marvelous things.
—PSALM 98:1

Joyous, Righteous, Risen Lord,

You have done marvelous things Lord. You have delivered your servants into freedom. You are victorious, vindicating your blessed America from our torturous struggles. You remembered your steadfast love for us and judged us with righteousness. All the world has seen your victory.

America makes a joyful noise to you. We break forth in songs praising your holy name. We lift our lyres, our tambourines, our trumpets, and our horns to make glorious melodies. We sing your praises. The seas roar, the waves clap, and the winds sing together with us in joy at the presence of the Lord.

You come to us Lord and judge all of our iniquities with righteousness and steadfast love. You love us with such great tenderness and show compassion for our failings. You lift us up from the shadows, take us into your arms, and tenderly calm our fears. You heal our hearts and our wounds and talk gently to us about choosing the better way.

You are love in all its glory. O Lord, we sing joyful praises to your holy name. Together, we join the voices, instruments, and hearts of your community of loving persons in glorious worship and thanksgiving for your merciful and gracious love.

Guide and protect us always, O Lord. Amen

IT IS HIS HOLINESS

...They cried to the Lord and he answered them.
—PSALM 99:6

O Lord of Zion, Holy One, He Who Is Holy,

You are the Lord. You are the King. All people tremble and the earthquakes rumble at your awesome power, Lord God.

You are enthroned above the cherubim and exalted above heaven and earth.

You are the lover of justice, executing righteousness throughout all the world. Awesome and mighty are you Lord!

America worships at your footstool, for you are holy.

You answer the cries and the prayers of your servants, when we keep your decrees and your statutes.

You are a forgiving God; our avenger, making right all of our adversary's wrongdoings.

We extol you God and worship at your majestic mountain, for you are holy!

When we cry to you, you answer us, for your love is from everlasting to everlasting.

Praise God for his holiness. Amen

ENTER HIS GATES

*Make a joyful noise to the Lord. Worship the Lord with
gladness; come into his presence with singing.
Know that the Lord is God. It is he that made us, and we are
his; we are his people, and the sheep of his pasture.
Enter his gates with thanksgiving, and his courts with
praise. Give thanks to him, bless his name.
For the Lord is good; his steadfast love endures forever,
and his faithfulness to all generations.*
—PSALM 100:1-5

Heavenly Father,

Thank you for creating America as one nation under God.

We are your people and all that we have is from your hand.

All that is love, all that is good, all that is hope, and all that is truth is your gift to America.

Nothing can separate us from your eternal love.

We enter your gates with joyous thanksgiving and praise, knowing we are entering your steadfast love and faithfulness.

Praise be to our good God! Amen

PLEDGE YOUR INTEGRITY AND JUSTICE

No one who practices deceit shall remain in my house; no one who utters lies shall continue in my presence.
—PSALM 101:7

Sovereign Lord, Prince of Peace, Purveyor of Justice,

America dedicates our loyalty to your name Lord, for you are the creator of peace and justice within our lands.

From you we learn the way that is blameless. Let us take your statutes and your commandments to heart and live true to them.

Within our halls at home, at work, at school, and in government, let us walk with integrity and truth.

Let our eyes not be distracted by anything that is lowly and base. Let any perversity fall away from us for we hate the work of evil.

Lord, silence anyone who slanders us. Guide us away from arrogance, elitism, slander, or false pride.

Make sure that everyone who practices deceit or lies against America is discovered and brought into your light of justice.

We will tolerate no one and no act that harms our innocents and our gullible in any way.

Help us, Lord, to end wicked power and cut off the evildoers who wreak havoc on our promise and peace.

Help all who are blameless and who walk in your way to flourish in your sunlight.

Let the faithful in our lands receive your favor that they may live in fullness with you.

Let us live in your glorious city, Lord, where your reign is just and pure.

Praise be to our just King. Amen

ETERNAL HEALING KING

But you O Lord are enthroned forever; your name endures to all generations.
—PSALM 102:12

Mighty Healing God,

Hear our prayers O Lord, for America cries to you. Incline your face towards us and do not hide it in this day of distress when the silent enemy lurks like a thief in the night ready to kill the vulnerable. Give your speedy answer for what lies ahead. Let your healing power loose throughout our lands.

Our days pass like smoke with so much good whisked away by threatening clouds of doom. We feel dread in our bones and our heart is stricken with grief for what has passed and fear for what is yet to come. We sit quietly alone, unable to eat, unable to go out, unable to see our loved ones, and unable to breathe. Offer your healing miracles, Lord.

All day long the untethered squawkers drone on, driving more and more fear into our lives. We live in uncertainty, barely able to find truth spoken from any corner. We watch with grief the growing death toll in cities across the world and at home. No one is left unaffected. People look to blame someone, anyone, for this devastating crisis.

Don't let us wither away like grass Lord. You are the forever King, enthroned from generation to generation. Rise up with compassion and spread your healing favor everywhere. Send the invisible enemy underground, never to harm again. Send answers to dissolve the take-over. Send your sun back into our darkened lives, that we may breathe free again.

You laid the foundations of life on earth. You created the generations. You spread the realm of heaven across your people to shelter, protect, and save us. You endure forever. Year over year, across millennia, you are the same. Wield your mighty healing power now as in ages of old. Make your servants whole, well, and happy that our children will live secure in your love, and our offspring shall be established in your name.

Come now Lord! Come and bring your mighty healing! Amen

GOD'S GREAT GOOD

*Bless the Lord, O my soul, and all that
is within me, bless his holy name.*
—PSALM 103:1

Blessed Lord, Giver of All Good Blessings,

Blessed and holy is your name,
Forgiver of all iniquities,
Healer of all diseases,
Redeemer for all lives,
Giver of all good things,
Vindicator for the oppressed,
King of justice,
Perpetrator of freedom,
Merciful and gracious,
Abounding in steadfast love,
Lover of our souls,
Ruler of heaven and earth,
Forgiver of all transgressions,
Father of all children,
Savior of all souls,
Everlasting to everlasting Spirit,
Righteous Lord for all generations,
Keeper of all wisdom.
There are not enough words to describe how great you are!

Let not America's iniquities rule over us.
Let not our blindness take our sense of good away.
Let not our ignorance convict us into poverty.
Let not our wrong mindedness make wrongful decisions.
Let not our sinful nature give over to self-interest.
Let not our arrogance rule our minds.
Let not our vulnerabilities lay open to attacks.

O Lord have dominion in the life of America.
We love you, for you are the one and only giver of life.
Thanks be to God for your everlasting goodness.

Amen

OUR PROVIDER

May my meditation be pleasing to him, for I rejoice in the Lord.
—PSALM 104:34

Heavenly Father, Awesome God,

America prays for the grace to marvel at your ongoing creation.
We pray for the grace of gratitude for your gifts of creation that bless our world.

Let all that we are praise the Lord.
Let all our thoughts be pleasing to the Lord.
Let us see with Jesus' eyes your wonder, splendor, and majesty.

When we breath the air, fill our lungs with wonder at your provision for all of our needs.
When we watch the birds of the sky, let us see the wonder of your creation.

Let us see the perfection of all things made by your Word: mountains grand, seas abundant, winds commanding, sun's reign, and moon's march.

Thank you for your glorious creation that homes America.
Thank you for your hands that feed us day by day.
Thank you for your Word that sustains us.

Thank you for your abundance that blesses us.
Thank you for your love that honors and protects us.
Thank you for our ancestry that grounds and enriches us.

O Lord, how majestic and beautiful you are!
You set the world right by your hand, all things in order and in place as they should be!

May all your creation praise your holy name, Lord!
May all your created ones serve and love one another in your image!

Praise be to our Creator God! Amen

OUR FAITHFUL GOD

Seek the Lord and his strength; seek his presence continually.
—PSALM 105:4

Lord of Tomorrow,

America is the remnant of your people; we are what remains from so many generations of faithful believers.
We are the ones who know, love, and serve you and your people.
Empower us Lord and enable us to carry on your lasting legacy.

Do not let false prophets and false leaders gain rule any longer.
Do not let the deceivers have their way.
Do not let those blind to the truth be led by those empty of truth.

Let your remnant have its day Lord.
Let your chosen commander take charge to lead in a way pleasing to you.
Let your legacy find its tomorrow forever.

Douse the mudslingers' message in mud to silence them.
Reveal the foolish who sow derision, so they disintegrate into nothing.
Divide the dividers to decimate their power and render them powerless.

Have it your way Lord, for your way is the best way always.
Have it your way, our Savior and Redeemer.
Have it your way, the only path to life eternal.

Let truth prevail Lord.
Let only your truth prevail, we pray.
Place your hand across this land to set all things right.

Thank you for your faithfulness from generation to generation.
Amen

CONFESS YOUR SINS

...He remembered his covenant and showed compassion according to the abundance of his steadfast love.
—PSALM 106:45

Confessor God,

Israel's story of your nation-building and saving grace is one that never dies, for it lives in perpetuity within America to this day. People fall from grace with evil acts and you lift them up again and again.

America has committed sin after sin - atrocious acts - and profaned your holy name. People in our borders deny you, worship your adversary, sacrifice our children, oppress our faithful, and lead us onto paths of self-destruction with distorted and tarnished claims of helping humanity.

We don't deserve what you have given us, how you free us, forgive us, and redeem us. You see the beauty of your creation and how the evil one perpetuates his bloodlust, and you have compassion on us. You are bent on saving us with your dependable love.

While America was founded to be a great nation, too many in our midst profane us and seek our destruction. Again, and again you save us from the pit, for our destruction is not your aim. You only want the best for us. You see the battle waging within us to remove the adversary's lair, and you have mercy on us.

The burdens we carry for provoking your anger weigh heavy on America. It tatters our flag, destroys our cities, sickens our people, and increases the downtrodden. Yet there are those within our borders who desire the very best, raise our flag high, help our people, extend generosity and aid, and worship you.

Empower your faithful people this day Lord, those working for a better America, a freer America, a more lovely America, worthy of our birthright and our name. Just as you have saved the Israelites for millennia with miraculous works because of your everlasting covenant, save America to live out our bright future for eons to come.

Help our people choose our leaders rightly, those in your image, who love us, want to flourish us, want to build us up, set us free, and give opportunities for living well here in our borders. Open eyes, open ears, and open hearts for all people to see what is right, what is true, and what is good when they bend their knee to you and let you in.

You are a gracious and forgiving God. O, how great you are! Amen

BOOK V

Inspired by PSALMS 107-150

The fifth book of Psalms is about how <u>God is among us.</u>

Let them thank the Lord for his steadfast love, for his wonderful works to humankind. For he satisfies the thirsty, and the hungry he fills with good things.
—PSALM 107:8

Engaging These Prayers

Jesus often said, "The kingdom is at hand." This refers to God being ever-present; he always with us. Consider how God is among us.

Here are some prompts:

- How does God demonstrate his presence?
- How can you know God is there?
- How does God inspire you to trust him?
- How can you pray for God to be with America?

God is ever-present; he is always with us. He is there, ready to make himself known to us. I like to say that his welcome sign is always on the door. His invitation is always open. It's up to you to knock and ask to come in. As Jesus says, "Ask and it will be given to you;

search and you will find; knock and the door will be opened to you." —Matthew 7:7

God is with you. He will never leave you or forsake you, as long as you don't deny him. Just remember that this is a relationship that requires both parties to be active for it to grow and thrive. As the relationship grows, so does the trust. It is a different kind of relationship, because you have to go inside yourself to your heart center to find him. You have to fill your heart with God's Word, so you come to know him and his love for you.

When you search for God, you will find him. You have to look beyond what is presented to your seeing eyes and use all of your senses, even your sixth sense, to come to know God. Walking in the Word helps you open your eyes to him. It perfectly describes his character and his loving ways.

If you aren't sure about your relationship with God, or that he is always with you, follow Jesus' simple formula. Ask God to make his presence known to you. Search for the signs of his daily miracles – when you look and listen for them you will find them. Knock and ask God to welcome you into his sanctuary. He welcomes you joyously. He celebrates every soul who finds their way to him. You will know when your joy is increased that you are with him.

TROUBLES BE GONE

Let them thank the Lord for his steadfast love, for his wonderful works to humankind.
—PSALM 107:8

The One Whose Love Endures Forever,

When America wanders in the desert wasteland, you feed us and keep us alive.

When we are oppressed, enslaved, and treated cruelly, you free us with acts of wonder.

When we can't find our way, you find us.

When we cry to you in our distress, you answer us.

When we are thirsty and parched, you quench our thirst.

When we are imprisoned in doom and gloom, miserable in chains and irons, you save us and break our bonds asunder.

When we are swallowed up by the rolling waves of life, you pull us up from drowning.

When we are buried under the rubble of broken dreams, you rescue us.

When plagues crouch at our door, you defeat them.

When murderers with smiling faces entice us, you block them.

When we only see darkness, you give us light.

When we are at our wits end, you send us hope.

When we are near death, you sit with us and hold us.

No matter what happens to us, you pull us into your loving arms.

In you there is everlasting hope, peace, and joy.

Your dedicated love endures forever.

Praise God for his wonderful loving ways and saving grace. Amen

SWEET VICTORY

O grant us help against the foe, for human help is worthless. With God, we shall do valiantly, it is he who will tread down our foes.
—PSALM 108:12-13

Lord of Victory,

America's heart is steadfast, O God, it is steadfast. We sing our hearts out in tune to your frequency of love, peace, and joy. We make glorious music with trumpets and violins, flutes and drums to awaken the dawn of this new day, the dawn of hope within the world.

We give thanks to you Lord, for you are merciful and gracious, pouring out your kindness from generation to generation. Your love is brighter than heaven's sun, moon, and stars. Your faithfulness reaches the clouds and wraps around heaven and earth.

America exalts you, Lord, above the heavens, the highest of the high. We see your glorious reign over all the earth. From your hand comes victory in answer to our prayers, and you rescue all whom you love. Your arms sustain the sanctity of life. Your way of living gives life everlasting.

Bring us into your sanctuary, O God. Let heaven's armies win the age-old battle of good over evil. Let your will prevail overall, that we may come to your time of everlasting peace. Seal your adversary, and all of his germs and pawns who steal life, in the vault of nevermore.

Thank you, victorious One. Amen

VINDICATE AMERICA

But you, O Lord my Lord, act on my behalf for your name's sake; because your steadfast love is good, deliver me.
—PSALM 109:21

Father of Grace,

The attacker is on all sides, moving silently and stealthily into America's public squares, business establishments, children's schools, home sanctuaries, and yes, even into our bodies. It is the evil one's invisible enemy with devastating outcomes for our most vulnerable. Life is upside down. No one lives the same today as yesterday.

We are pressed in, stamped down, shaken up, and turned on our head, with our human connections completely disrupted. The very things our people need as humans - touch, hugging, conversation, companionship, worship - usurped by the enemy as ways to disperse his evil snares. Our life has stopped, our hallways are empty, and our people have dispersed into their cocoons to fight the attacker's spread.

Never have we seen anything like this. Never have we encountered a time where human connection is the thing that wields the evil one's sword on our life. Nothing seems real. Reality has shifted with isolation and rampant fear becoming the norm. Where are you Lord? Can we count on you now, because we need you more than ever? Are you seeing this? Are you with us? Is the flood coming again to purge the evil all around us? Will we survive this?

Oh yes! There you are. You're in the faces of the caregivers throughout our lands providing care for our needs. You're in the minds of scientists working to stem the deluge. You're in the hearts of leaders meeting daily to plan, prepare, and decide on the next best steps for our safety. You're in the actions of our young people organizing food drives for the elderly and vulnerable. You're calling forward the best of us, to rise up and help others. Oh yes! That is you, Lord!

You move the best in us to action Lord. At your command, people rise up to your higher call. At your command, people use our hands, hearts, and minds to act in the ways you taught us. You shield and protect your people because you need them as much as they need you. For you created us, you taught us, you pursued us, you love us, and we are your greatest prize. We are your image-bearers.

For your name's sake, you act on our behalf. Your steadfast love is good, and you deliver us. People will know it is by your power that we live to praise another day. It is by your hand that your beloved America will weather this plague and be stronger and more united than ever.

Thanks be to God, who vindicates his beloved! Amen

GOD'S VICTORIOUS KING

*The Lord says to my Lord, "Sit at my right hand
until I make your enemies your footstool."*
—PSALM 110:1

Victorious Priestly King Jesus,

America sings praises to you, for you are our priestly King.
You sit at the right hand of God the Father Almighty.
God makes your enemies your footstool, for no enemy can stand against you.

You send your scepter and sword from your Zion mount, wielding its power to heal, and disrupting evil power structures.
Your rule is higher than your foes' evil intentions.

No enemy can hide from your forces of good to save lives.
We turn ourselves over to you, offering ourselves willingly, as you lead your legions from the holy mount.

You come on God's forever promise, to bring your saving grace.
You come with God at your back; all authority given to you.
You shatter kings of evil empires; and dismantle nation-states terrorizing their people.

No head of evil anywhere on earth shall stand against you.
No one who worships your adversary, practices evil arts, or carries bloodlust in their hearts will keep their head, for they will roll before you.

When you have reclaimed America, and your kingdom world-wide, you will kneel by the stream, and drink the clear, pure water.
You will lift your head and smile, knowing that all is well in the kingdom of God.

By the saving blood of Jesus, all is well.

Praise be to our victorious Savior King. Amen

CYNTHIA J STEWART

WORKS OF WONDER

I will give thanks to the Lord with my whole heart.
—PSALM 111:1

Gracious and Merciful Lord,

Praise the Lord, America! Give thanks to the Lord with everything that is within you. Give thanks. Stand with the community of beloved persons, the congregation of believers, and the community of saints to give God your honor and praise.

For great is our Lord. Great are the works of his hands that paint the morning skies, lift the birds in delightful songs, and raise the flower faces to his glory. His works reveal his honor and majesty on offer to his beloved people. See how his righteousness is trustworthy and true, enduring forever.

All that the Lord has done is life-giving and life-affirming, letting us know how wonderful he is, how gracious, merciful, and kind he is. All that we have is from our Lord. All food, shelter, healing, and gifts of life are from his hand. He promises us this and so much more when we walk with him and live according to his precepts.

He birthed America and gave us a heritage of long-lasting goodness. He shows through the power of his just works and his healing grace that in his hands we stand, united and strong. Life is joyful and love-filled when we live by his commandments, laws, and precepts. He gives us the Book of Truth full of wisdom in how to live life abundantly in the sunshine of his love.

His way of life is established for evermore for the upright and the faithful. He gives redemption to fulfill his lasting covenant when we stand with him. May we hold you in awe Lord, that we may gain understanding and wisdom of how to live in your light and spread your light into the world.

Holy and awesome are you. Holy is your name. May we glorify your name for evermore for you are more than worthy of our praise.

Glorify our awesome God! Amen

RIGHTEOUS BLESSINGS

Happy are those who fear the Lord...They rise in the darkness as a light for the upright; they are gracious, merciful, and righteous.
—PSALM 112:1,4

Everlasting Father,

When America seeks you and acts according to your commandments for living well, you give us a wealthy life, full of goodness, light, and grace. Our descendants will be mighty throughout our lands and will receive your continual blessings.

Our home is full of your happiness. Our life is abundant in family, love, and blessings. Our righteousness shall endure forever, through all our generations. Justice is our bellwether by which we conduct all our affairs.

We are upright in shining light into the darkness, helping others, and doing and acting as you do, Lord, loving and benefitting everyone. We rise higher than the darkness, and are gracious, merciful, and generous. All is well with us.

We are steadfast and will never be moved from your rock. From generation to generation we are sought after for sanctuary. We are remembered for our compassion for eternity. Our good acts will live in the minds of people for generations to come.

Though evil tidings darken our door, threaten our people, and herald warnings of doom and death, our hearts are secure in you Lord. Day by day we win in many ways, and with your help, we will triumph over our foes, unafraid and powerful.

We go about freely, giving aid to the afflicted, goods to the poor, and lifting up the downtrodden. Our justice, mercy, and grace inform our leaders, our doctors, and our workers in how to be wise in their judgments. Your way of being, thinking, and doing endures and good prevails.

We stand through it all Lord, because we greatly delight in your commandments. Those who stand with us will prevail.

Praise be to our Lord, our victor and our Savior! Amen

KING OF LOVE

*He raises the poor from the dust, and lifts the needy from
the ash heap, to make them sit with princes...*
—PSALM 113:7,8

Lord God of All Heaven and Earth,

Praise the Lord!
America, servant of the Lord, praise the Lord!
America praises you Lord for your name is glorious and wonderful.
There is no one like you!

Blessed is your name, may your name be forever praised.
Who is more glorious than you, the one who created us?
The sun rises, the moon circles, and the stars sparkle in honor of you.

You are the highest of the high, above all nations and principalities.
Your glory fills heaven and earth, blessing all your creation.
May your name be praised from morning to night.

You are Prince among princes, ruling with valor, honor, and righteousness.
Seated on your blessing mount, ruling from on high, you view all happenings in heaven and earth with piercing clarity.
You see the lowly and raise their tear-stained faces from the dust.

You see the needy and lift their weakness from the ashes of their lives.
You place your lowly believers among the princes, honoring each one as a child of God.
No one shall live barren in your kingdom, for all will birth the joyous blessings of life with you in your family of loving persons.

All praise and honor to you, Lord, for you are the King of love!
Praise the Lord forevermore! Amen

WONDROUS EXODUS

Tremble, O earth, at the presence of the Lord...
—PSALM 114:7

Majestic Father, God of Wonder and Might,

America sees your miraculous works! Even the seas flea at your command, rivers turn back, mountains rumble, and hills shake. For you created everything and you command it all to save us.

Yet your mission is not to control, your mission is to liberate. You destined to save your America and you have worked your redeeming grace throughout time, in the lives of your beloved people.

Do not forsake us for our iniquities, though they are numerous. Remember your covenant to redeem us and save us from our bad choices, misguided thinking, arrogant ways, and self-serving hands.

Give us a path forward that pushes back the troubled waters, leaves our persecutors behind in the rolling waves, confuses the godless, and makes you the victor.

Call your earth and all its elements into action to save your America, land of the free, and home of the brave. We are on the march to Zion to live with you in your glorious land, in peace, hope, and love.

O how we love you Lord! Amen

WORTHLESS IDOLS

May you be blessed by the Lord, who made heaven and earth.
—PSALM 115:15

O Lord, Father of All,

From your hands flow all of America's blessings.
From you, O God, comes life, love, and peace.
From you comes the means to live and flourish.
From you we receive our families and our friends.

Nothing that is good in our life comes from anyone but you.
In you we place our faith and trust to guide us through trying times.
You heal us in all our suffering, illnesses, diseases, and curses.
You are the God of love who sees and hears us, speaks and walks with us.

It is you that guides us day by day from the realms of heaven.
Though we have great things available to make a better life, nothing is more wonderful than your love and companionship.
If we make idols and trust in them, we receive nothing in return.
Nothing our hands make with silver and gold is more precious than you God.

Direct our leaders in their decision-making for our future.
Stay with our people and open all eyes to see what is real.
Open all minds to you, O God, who made heaven and earth.
Open all hearts to you, O God, who increases blessings for our children, generation to generation.

You are our help and our shield.
Help us move through this day in a way that glorifies you.
Help us do better today than yesterday.
Let us trust in you and you alone.

Praise be to God the Father of all blessings. Amen

ALWAYS THERE

Return, O my soul, to your rest, for the Lord has dealt bountifully with you.
—PSALM 116:7

Gracious Provider,

Time and again Americans offer our prayers and ask for your hand upon our lives.
You never fail in your love and provision for us and our families.
You are always there for us because you love us.
You give and give and give more.

When there is no one to turn to, you offer your hand.
When there is no answer, you provide it.
When all looks bleak, you shed your light.
When our hearts are downcast, you lift us up.

When we are sick, you heal us.
When we need your help, you provide your aid.
When we are bound, you break our bonds.
When we are depressed, you lift our hearts.

You hear our requests and incline your ear to us.
Only you fill our needs in ways unexpected and miraculous.
What shall we return to you Lord for all your goodness to us?
How can we thank you enough for your merciful ways?

We will offer our vows and sing your praises aloud.
We will make known that you are the one true provider.
We will dedicate our lives to learning your wisdom ways.
We will praise you as the one and only giver of life everlasting.

We sing your praises to thank you for putting our souls at rest.
Thank you for your wisdom guiding leaders around the world.
Thank you for your healing grace pouring into all lives.
Thank you for your mercies, new every morning.

Thank you, magnificent God. Amen

WORSHIP HIM

Praise the Lord, all you nations! Extol him, all you peoples! For great is his steadfast love toward us, and the faithfulness of the Lord endures forever.
—PSALM 117:1-2

Praise the Lord, praise the Lord!

Every cell of our bodies praises the Lord.
Every thought of our minds praises the Lord.
Every wish of our hearts praises the Lord.
Every word of our mouths praises the Lord.
Every act of our hands praises the Lord.
Every part of us praises the Lord.

Extol the Lord.
Laud the Lord.
Exalt the Lord.
Every being praises the Lord.
Every animal praises the Lord.
Every plant praises the Lord.
Every sunset praises the Lord.

Let all that lives, praise the Lord.
Let all the sunrises and sunsets speak to his glory.
Let all the stars and universes reveal his majesty.
Let all the flowing waters sing out his wonder.
Let all the world and all the earth give him glorious praise.
Let forgiveness rise like the sun, healing all hurts and pains.
Let this day give you your just praise Lord!

Thank you for everything. Amen

VICTORY SONGS

This is the day the Lord has made, let us rejoice and be glad in it.
—PSALM 118:24

O Lord Victorious,

Victory in all its forms comes from your hand, for your love endures throughout all time. America is a beautiful nation and our strength leads the world in good for all people. Let our people unite in the principles that make us great: life, liberty, and justice.

America prays for legions of angels to help the afflicted and shield the strong, for we know you will provide them wherever they are needed. May your hand shield your people as in days of old that the plague will pass over so they may keep their lives.

May you loosen the bonds of isolation and give your people freedom to pursue their purpose and their good. May you wield justice for all people that peace and prosperity will prevail.

When we are distressed, we need only to seek you, for you supply us peace. With you at our side we have no fear, for you are there to help us. In you Lord, we find refuge and rest. In you and you alone, we place our confidence.

When trouble presses in on us, you strengthen us to push it away, for you are our mighty salvation. You lift us up and give us success in defeating our hidden enemies. By your will evil is pushed down and good rises up across our nation.

Open your gates of homecoming Lord that we may come home to give you thanks. We give you praise for you are so good. Your name is forever; your love is steadfast and true. Your works are full of honor and majesty.

How faithful you are Lord. Your sovereignty covers the earth and America bows down to your greatness. We sing praises to your name and seek your will that we may glorify you.

Praise be to God the victorious! Amen

GLORIOUS LAW

Happy are those whose way is blameless, who walk in the law of the Lord.
—PSALM 119:1

Author of Life,

Happy are Americans when we keep your laws and your decrees and walk in your way.
Pour your Word into our hearts where it may remain as our guide in all that we do.
Fix our eyes on your commandments and statutes and give us your righteous ordinances to direct our paths.
Help us keep our ways pure, according to your Word.

May we treasure your Word in our heart that it may bring us gladness.
Teach us your statutes that we may share in your blessings, Lord.
Give us your ordinances that we may declare them in the public square.
Let us not forget your glorious truths revealed in your Word, that we may live according to your promises.

Be with our loved ones throughout this land.
Hold them close with your wings and protect their health and safety.
Walk with the thousands of those on the frontlines and give them strength and comfort in fighting the scourge.
Let us plant our purpose in you to bring you glory and praise for fulfilling our hearts desires for love and happiness.

Thank you for this day with you! Amen

THE TRUTH-TELLER

In my distress I cry to the Lord, that he may answer me.
—PSALM 120:1

Lord of All, Deliverer of Peace,

Lying lips all around. Lying lips all around, Lord.
Deceitful tongues hurling black coals that ignite rumors and fears.
America feels alien in our home hearing all the contemptuous lies about us. Lies about our honorable intentions. Lies about our honorable past.
Why, Lord? Why so many lies?
We search for truth in the public square. There is none. Who can we trust?
Who that is informing, instructing, and directing us can be trusted Lord?
Why do so many want to lie, generate fear, confuse people, insight panic, and promote war-like actions?
Has everyone lost their way? Where are the truth-tellers?
Where is your truth Lord?

I am your God. My truth is within you America.
My words are true and trustworthy.
Stay close to me.
Read my words, forever true, forever real, forever righteous.
Call my Spirit to you and listen...listen...listen.
Quiet your mind and have courage.
My Spirit will instruct you in all truths.
You will know by the peace and calm you feel what is truthful.
Listen to my Spirit. I give you discernment to sort the truth from the lies.
I give you knowing for what to believe.
I give you all that you need to know when you need to know it to act righteously.

Hear me.
Have courage.
Be strong.
Bring peace.

Yes Lord, yes, yes, Lord! You are trustworthy and true.
Praise be to you, majestic truth-teller, deliverer of peace. Amen

GOD'S PROTECTION

My help comes from the Lord, who made heaven and earth.
—PSALM 121:2

Our Lord, Our Keeper, Our Helper,

All help comes from you Lord.

Where else need America look for aid but to you? You are our keeper and helper. You do not slumber or sleep for your presence is always with us.

You are our shade to protect us from the piercing sun and the waxing moon. You keep us from all evil. You hold our life in your hands.

When we go out or come in, you keep us now and tomorrow. We have you to protect and guide us and in you we trust. You are our true source of help and always alert to our needs.

We give ourselves freely to you, Lord. We rise with the sun, sing your praise, and set about your work for the day. At day's end we lie down and give joyous thanksgiving for a beautiful day.

Wherever we go or whatever we do, you are there, our Savior, protector, and shield. As we set about this day, we give it to you Lord, that we may accomplish much and fulfill our royal purpose in you.

Keep America, its people, and the world safe in your hands today Lord, especially those caring for and serving others who are suffering and isolated.

Thank you, Lord for your loving protection. Amen

PRAISES FROM AMERICA

For the sake of my relations and friends, I will say, "Peace be within you."
—PSALM 122:8

God of Zion, Our Stronghold, Our Peace Giver,

America is glad to hear your invitation to come in.

We stand at your gate and knock. We hope that we may be in your presence, in the heart of your just rule, to give you thanks.

We gladly pray for peace for the world, starting with peace in our own hearts.

We find peace only within your walls and security within your gaze, O Lord, for the hidden demons are all around us driving fear and panic.

May those with evil intent shrink at your feet and fall at the sight of you.

May those who are misguided by wrong ideas, see your peaceful face, hear your loving tones, and embrace your righteous truths.

May those who fear the future be shown your promise of tomorrow.

All that is good and powerful is within your gates, bring us under your towering presence, Lord.

Show us your great love and mercy.

Show us there is nothing to fear. Let us turn it all over to you, for you are in full charge.

For our sake and for our future, reveal to us the good ahead.

May we feel your deep and abiding peace and love, and know that in you, all is well.

Your loving mercy abides forever. Let us abide in you and share your great love now and forevermore.

Within your will we live secure. Amen

MERCY PLEASE

*Have mercy upon us, O Lord, have mercy upon us, for
we have had more than enough of contempt.*
—PSALM 123:3

Majestic King, Prince of Peace, Merciful God,

America lifts up our eyes to you, O Lord, on heaven's throne where you reign in goodness and truth.

As your servants, here to serve you and your people, we look for your everlasting protection and strength in these perilous times.

Have mercy on us, won't you Lord, just as you promised?

For those with great contempt strive for our very destruction because of our thriving powers of love and goodness.

Our souls are downtrodden and weary of all the contempt, ill-will, and evil actions.

Breathe life into us and lift our souls to fight with you in this epic spiritual battle of life over death, good over evil, and heaven over hell.

Give us your mercy, your grace, and your armor to win the day, awaken hearts and minds for good, and live through this cataclysmic reset of the world as we know it.

In your mercy and grace, we live strong and free forevermore.

In God and God alone, we trust! Amen

ONLY YOU LORD

Our help is in the name of the Lord who made heaven and earth.
—PSALM 124:8

O Creator, Our God, Our Redeemer,

Who can save America from the snares of the world except for you Lord?

Who can save America from the evil one who plots our demise except for you Lord?

If you are not on our side, who can save us from the enemy when their anger is kindled against us?

Who can save America from being swallowed up by the raging torrents, clashing waves, torrential storms, consuming floods, or pervasive onslaught? Only you Lord!

When all is bleak, when all is dark, when we are on our knees, it is you Lord who comes on wings of angels to give us freedom and life!

You Lord are our Redeemer and our Savior.

You made heaven and earth. Our help comes from you. Only you!

Nothing before us is bigger than you, God, standing behind us!

Thank you, Lord, for all the ways you redeem us.

Make way for the Lord! Alleluia! Amen

CYNTHIA J STEWART

PRECIOUS SECURITY

*Those who trust in the Lord are like Mount Zion,
which cannot be moved, but abides forever.*
—PSALM 125:1

O Lord, God of The Mount,

You are Mount Zion - strong, unmoving, unshakeable - America's tower of security.

You created the mountains across America, just as you did for Jerusalem, in honor of your serenity and grace.

Trusting in you, we enter your security where evil neither has sway nor corrupts.

The hidden, pervasive, and stealthy scepter of wickedness and death may never live in the land you have set aside for the righteous.

We pray that you will give grace to the faithful, those who praise your name and walk humbly in your way.

We know we can trust you to protect us, provide for us, and flourish us, in all times no matter what is happening in the world.

May America be your strong mount bringing your towering security to the world.

May we be among your good people doing your good work, and only your good work, in the world.

Praise God for your everlasting mercy and grace. Amen

JOYOUS HARVEST

When the Lord restored the fortunes of Zion, we were like those in a dream.
—PSALM 126:1

King of the Harvest,

When you restore America's most treasured possessions, our families and children, we will see your kingdom come to earth. You will fulfill our closest-held dream that your will be done, and full harvest will come.

The joyous sounds of laughter will fill our halls in festive celebrations from dusk to dawn. No heart will escape the glorious wonder of your almighty presence. No soul will go unfilled by your gracious Spirit.

Your resurrected Son's face will beam love-signals to all who've come from the harvest. Everyone will sing together in honor and praise of you. Together we shall rejoice and praise your holy name.

America walks with Jesus on his last sojourn through darkness, torment, and isolation. The darkness has not passed, it will consume us first, just as it did Jesus. We know, as he knows, you are at our side and will carry us through it all.

You are the King of the harvest and at your word, the darkness is overcome. You will restore all fortunes from your storehouses of goodness. You will send your workers into the plentiful harvest to reap your good fruits with shouts of joy.

May those who go out weeping to spread your seed for sowing, come home with shouts of joy. May your workers yield a great harvest of souls. Everyone will sing together in honor and praise of you. Together we shall rejoice and praise your holy name.

CYNTHIA J STEWART

O King of harvest, please carry your community of loving persons through the darkness on the day of reckoning into the resurrection, just as you carried your Son, our Lord. Give us the day of your glory, merciful God.

Gracious is our God, abounding in forever love! Amen

THE BLESSING OF CHILDREN

Unless the Lord builds the house, those who build it labor in vain.
—PSALM 127:1

Giver of Life, Hearth, and Home,

Unless the Lord builds America, its builders labor in futility.
Unless the Lord grows the family, parents with kids live in strife.
Unless the Lord guards us, the night guards watch in blindness.

If we rise early, work for ourselves, and lie down late, our work never ends.
If we worry all day, hold our cares from the Lord, our worries consume our nights.
If we run our own life, ignoring the Lord's commands, we run ourselves into despair.

Let the Lord build our house, grow our family, give us purpose, and cover our needs, so that we may rest peacefully at night.
The Lord gives everything to his beloved.
Our children are the heritage of the Lord, and the greatest reward he gives to us.

The Lord loves all children as he loved his Son.
The Lord loves and blesses our children and families.
As God would have it, children bring blessings and security to all generations.

When America's homes are full of children, there is great happiness and joy.
When children thrive and flourish, the future is bright.
When Americans love and protect our children, God brings abundant life forevermore.

God bless America Lord, protect our hearth and home, and give our children your brightest future.

Thank you, Lord. Amen

CYNTHIA J STEWART

LIFE IN GOD

Happy is everyone who fears the Lord, who walks in his ways.
— PSALM 128:1

Gracious God, Faithful Father,

You give America life and give it abundantly when we walk in your ways;
For your ways reveal how life is best lived in happiness.

You desire that we be happy walking with you all the days of our lives.
You desire that we be rewarded by the fruits of our labors, when we grow in the fruits of your Spirit.

You desire that we be loved, by our family, friends, and co-laborers, just as you love us.
You desire that our table be full, our children and family surrounding us.

Magnificent Lord, you shower great blessings on America.
When we walk in your ways, we learn meaning, purpose, service, and love, and our hearts are full.

May we see prosperity all the days of our lives, knowing it is from your hand.
May we live according to your Word all the days of our lives that we may fulfill our destiny in you.

May we follow your light through threatening darkness to see our children's children.
May we rejoice in the coming of your Son to fulfill your everlasting promises.

Thank you, gracious God, for our happy lives. Amen

HE IS RIGHTEOUS

The Lord is righteous; he has cut the cords of the wicked.
— PSALM 129:4

Righteous Lord, God of Zion,

Zion is the seat of your just rule Lord, from which all good and all justice flows.

Your reign is good, Lord, yet so many hate you. They are deaf, dumb, and blind to your ways; they cannot see or hear you. Their hearts are shallow for the lack of your Spirit. Their thoughts and ways are hypocritical and their actions conflict with their words. They sow confusion and distrust that leads to despair and destruction.

Though they have attacked America from our early beginnings, they have not prevailed in destroying us. They have done terrible things to our people, our women and children, as well as those who have sought our sanctuary. In your righteousness, you cut the cords of the wicked, revealing their true aims, putting them to shame, and giving them their just due.

Across all time you have ruled with justice and goodness, mercy and grace. You ask for people to love one another and to love you first and foremost, that they may find love at their own center from which to carry on your purposes. You ask for people to come with you, follow your ways, that they may have joy and peace throughout their lives.

Let us put ourselves at the foot of Zion on our knees to hand over our lives and service to your good ends. We pray that those who love you may rule America, for you have given your people victory after victory when they put truth, reason, and justice to work for all people in America.

May those who see and hear your call carry it forward to prosper your people with love and goodness, safety and protection. May they be your face and your hands in serving your people. May they know the depth and the breadth of your steadfast love.

Praise God of righteousness and justice! Amen

WE WAIT

I wait for the Lord, my soul waits, and in his word I hope.
—PSALM 130:5

Redeemer Lord,

From the depth of our beings, Americans cry to you. Hear our voices and turn your countenance upon us. Let our prayers reach you, Almighty One. We wait for you and hope in your Word until our soul is satisfied.

America waits for your redeeming grace, for in you exists the only power to redeem us. For you do not count all our iniquities, though they wrap the globe round and round, enough to strangle all in its path. We wait for your forgiveness.

You know us and know our promises. We revere you for your forgiveness. We wait for you and hope in your word. We wait for you, more than the dawn of the new day or the promise of tomorrow. We wait because we trust in you.

You created people in your image, and you know they are little sheep that must be tended to, little children that must be loved, comforted, taught, and rebuked. We wait for you to grow us in Christ's image.

Your love is steadfast, unswerving, undying, and undaunted. We can hope in you to redeem all our iniquities. Our hope is not lost in you, for your power and your promise to redeem is steadfast. We wait for you to free us Lord.

Even in the public square where divisions form deep crevasses and polarize people, where the attackers shout lies and act in violence seeking to dominate with hate, even there you bring redemption. We wait for your redeeming grace Lord.

Let your glory shine into the public square and change the hearts of the untethered attackers. End the bitterness and heal the hearts that divide, the hearts that are broken and grieving, and the hearts that are downtrodden. We wait for your healing mercies.

Redeemer God, we wait for you. Amen

EVER TRUSTING YOU

Hope in the Lord from this time on and forevermore.
—PSALM 131:3

Almighty God, Trustworthy and True,

America does not need to rule the world, or to be dictator of humankind. We do not need to be in places where we have no business. We do not need to fantasize grandiose plans to wield our power and influence.

We have our own business to tend to, our own people to care for. We need only to stand our ground, to stand firm on our foundations, and to be the true model of life, liberty, and justice.

We need only to cultivate a quiet heart, like a babe in its mother's arms, calm, quiet, and peaceful in our souls. Peace begins within our souls. Our soul at peace acts in your image.

We wait for you Lord, to hear your Word. We hope in you Lord, today, tomorrow. and forevermore. We trust in you Lord, for your Word is the rock on which we stand.

Come, Lord of divine hope, come! Amen

OUR ETERNAL LORD

Rise up, O Lord, and go to your resting place!
—PSALM 132:8

O Lord God, the Almighty One,

Your promises are true and trustworthy, lasting for eternity.
Your covenants are fulfilled for all time.
For you swore an oath to King David, a prophecy of your Son to come and sit on the majestic throne of life everlasting.
You prepared a lamp for your anointed one, the Lord Jesus, whose crown gleams bright and beautiful.
He has kept your covenants, fulfilled his mission, conquered death for all, rose from the depths of the deep, carried the sins of the world, and now sits on his rightful throne next to you.

You chose Zion as your eternal home, your forever place.
You bless its provisions, satisfy its poor, clothe its priests with salvation, and its faithful with joyous lives.
Your everlasting rule is gracious and merciful.
Your Son, our Lord Jesus, is our prince of peace, our divine Advocate.
You ask us to keep your covenant to love you above all and our neighbors as ourselves, so that you may welcome us into Zion where we will be blessed by you.

Lord may your Son reign supreme in our hearts and in our lives.
May we find our ways to Zion, step by step in one direction leading to you.
May we rejoice in the streets with shouts of joy as we glorify you.
May we bring America and all nations to kneel at your footstool.
What a glorious vision for us and our world!
May we welcome you into our midst moment to moment and praise your holy name forevermore.
May we give thanks for our Lord Jesus, our Savior, our King.

Thank you, Lord Jesus, for giving us life eternal. Amen

UNITY BLESSES

How very good and pleasant it is when kindred live together in unity.
—PSALM 133:1

Our God of Unity,

You desire us to be kindred souls, living together in unity, that we may have abundant lives.

Together we sustain the force of your greater presence; we can do more and live longer for the lack of strife and worry.

You unify us as one body in your church, each with special gifts to support the whole.

You bring peace in our unity allowing each one to give their highest and best.

You anoint us as your kindred spirits and provide for us in soft and gentle ways.

When we lay down our rhetoric and our weapons that divide and harm us, we benefit and win together.

Help us in this time of strife and isolation to pursue your promises of unity where good may flow so people may flourish.

Thank you for the blessing of unity. America together! Amen

ALL IS WELL

May the Lord, maker of heaven and earth, bless you from Zion.
—PSALM 134:3

Father of Blessed Goodness,

Come America!
Bless the Lord!
All you who serve our King, bless his name.
Yes, bless his holy name!

All who come through the night by the Lord's grace, bless the Lord!
Lift your hands to heaven, raise your voices in praise, come and bless the Lord!
Praise the Lord's goodness and his unshakeable love!
Praise the Lord and bless his holy name!

O Lord, maker of heaven and earth, send treasures from your blessing-mount in Zion.

Praise be to our God, for in your hands, all is well. Amen

ALMIGHTY GOODNESS

For I know that God is great; our Lord is above all gods.
—PSALM 135:5

Almighty God,

Praise the Lord, America!
Praise the name of the Lord!
Praise the miraculous works of God!
Give praise, all servants of God!
Priests in his sacred temple give praise!
Shepherds of his beloved flocks give praise!
Leaders in our halls of justice give praise!
Parents of little lambs give praise!
Shout alleluia for his great goodness!
Sing anthems to his beautiful name.

For the Lord has done great things for America for generations.
He brings liberty-seekers from many lands to freedom's shores.
He anoints leaders to protect our future with his righteous laws.
He gives wisdom to doctors, scientists, and inventors to heal us.
He sustains our liberties, handing freedom-fighters victory in wars near and far.
He raises the golden sun in skies of blue to light our work.
He paints crimson skies from east to west, to mark our rest.
He sends signs and wonders to show his enduring love.
Whatever pleases the Lord, he gives to us.
Praise the Lord for his boundless gifts of love!

Those who make their own gods and trust in them, end up like them: no eyes to see, no ears to hear, no breath in their mouths.
For those who love the Lord, his name endures forever and his renown for all time.
Throughout all ages, all crises, and all sufferings, God carries us!

The Lord vindicates his beloved America at every turn, giving endless compassion to our people.
In his hands, we rest in peace.

O America, bless the Lord! Praise his holy name! Amen

HIS LOVE

O give thanks to the Lord, for he is good, for his steadfast love endures forever.
—PSALM 136:1

Lord of Lords, God of Heaven,

America give thanks to the Lord for all his goodness!

His love endures forever.
His love is supreme.
His love is righteous.
His love is miraculous.
His love creates all.
His love is marvelous.
His love is endless.
His love is grounded.
His love is light filled.
His love gives life.
His love is hopeful.
His love is eternal.
His love is generous.
His love is for everyone.
His love is trustworthy.
His love is free.
His love is victorious.
His love is orderly.
His love is limitless.
His love is merciful.

God loves all, he gives all, and he is all we need.

Give thanks to the God of Heaven, for his love lasts forever. Amen

LAMENT FOR LOSS

"Sing us one of the songs of Zion!"
—PSALM 137:3

Lord of Peace,

On the banks of the river of loss, America sits and weeps.
We have lost much that is known to us, sitting in our isolation.
We have lost persons we love so dearly.
We have lost times with family and friends, hugging and kissing.
We have lost worshipping and singing your praises, in unity and love.
We have lost our jobs, our livelihoods, and our incomes.
We have lost times at schools, ballgames, and theatres.

"Sing songs to your all-powerful God now", the mockers taunt, for they do not know you.
Let us not forget the songs we've sung before, even in these foreign times.
Let us not forget you, O God, in these times of grief and loss.
Let us sit speechless, if we forget to sing your praises.
Let us forget our greatest joys, if we forget the good you have given us.
Let us sit in turmoil, if we forget your peaceful presence.
Let us not feel your joy, if we give up on you.

Never forget the Lord America, for he has not left you.
The Lord always comes to set things right again.
Keep the Lord forever on your mind, for his promises are trustworthy.
His plans are to prosper you, not to harm you, and to give you hope and a future.
Your loved ones are with him, in his tender care, so grieve no more.
Your days of joy are still ahead.
Let his peace come into your heart now and prepare to live the new future he has created for you.

You are our hope, Lord. Guide us through the darkness. Amen

SINCERE PRAISE

On the day I called, you answered me, you increased my strength of soul.
—PSALM 138:3

Royal Father, God of Promises,

America praises you Lord with our hearts full of joy.
Before those who aim to rule us, we sing vows only to you Lord.
We bow down to your holiness to praise and glorify your name.
For your bountiful love and unending faithfulness encompasses our existence.
Above all, we exalt your gracious name with unassailable power to protect and save us.
Above all, we exalt your incarnate Word with full trust, hope, and rejoicing.
When we call on you, you answer us, increasing our strength and courage.

May all people praise you O Lord, when they hear the words of your mouth sharing your great promises of hope.
May all people cling to your life-giving ways O Lord, for your glory is great, and your acts more wonderful than any king's.
Though you live in the highest heavens, you look lovingly upon the humble-hearted.
You recognize the troubling acts of the proud from afar, guarding your face from their gaze.
No matter the rushing waters swirling around us, you preserve our lives.
You stretch out your hand to save us from all enemies great and small; and you always fulfill your plans for us.

On these truths we can stand. Thanks be to God, our Father Almighty. Amen

INCREDIBLE GOD

Search me O God and know my heart...
—PSALM 139:23

God of Life and Love,

You search Americans and you know us, so much better than we know ourselves.
You see all and know all about us, our every action in pursuing our purpose to serve.
You know our comings and goings, for you are familiar with all our ways.
You perceive our every thought completely, and our words before they are spoken.

You are fully present with us; you are above, before, behind, and beside us.
You place your hands upon our shoulders, so we do not escape your loving care.
Knowing all that you know about us is too wonderful for us to comprehend or understand.
For you are our all in all, Lord, and you know and love us perfectly.

Your Spirit is pervasive and relentless; where can we go that you are not there?
Where can we flee from your presence found everywhere?
There is no hiding from you.
Your hand guides us, earth to heaven, east to west, and holds us fast in your inescapable supervision.

If we go up to the heavens, we find you there; or down to the depths of the earth, you are there.
If we ride the wings of dawn and settle on the far side of the seas, you are there.
If we cringe and hide in the darkness, you become the light for us to show our way home.

If we seek your face at dawn, you lift us up, to fly with you in the golden sunlight.

You created us from our inmost beings, tied with silver cords to you.
You knit us together from dust, in Mother earth's womb.
We praise you, for we are like no other nation on earth.
Like all your works, our nation is wonderful, glorious, and beautiful.

You framed America, pouring wondrous thoughts into our birthers' vision for us.
We were conceived with undying principles for freedom.
You imagined what we could be and gave deep insights and vision for us to become a shining lighthouse for the world.

You ordained all our days before us, recording them in the Book of Life.
How precious are your thoughts, O God, that we should be made a nation like none other!
How vast is the sum of them, that we should become your sheltering harbor!
How amazing it is that you are always with us, always have been, and always will be!

The constant rise of enemies within our land puzzles us, for we abhor those who rise up against you.
We pray that you slay the wicked forever, God.
May your long-standing patience with your enemies end now.
Silence those who blaspheme your holy name.

Search us and know everything that is within our hearts.
Test us, even our anxious and confused thoughts.
Remove any offensive way within us;
And lead us each day to our forever tomorrows,
In your kingdom of love.

Inescapable God, how we love you. Amen

DELIVER THE GOOD

*I know the Lord maintains the cause of the needy
and executes justice for the poor.*
—PSALM 140:12

God of Vengeance, Lord of Justice,

Deliver America from the evildoers within our camps.
Protect us from those conducting subterfuge against us,
And those who stir up wars in cyberspace, public health, and financial markets to weaken us.
They rattle and speak evil like pythons, spewing venom like vipers.

Guard us from wicked plots and plans to take-over America.
Protect us from the evil-worshippers seeking our downfall.
Warn us of the traps of slanderers who spread nets of lies to catch us in their snares.
Shield us from the betrayers who try to win our trust with lies.

O Lord, you are our God; give ear to the voice of our supplications.
You are our strong deliverer; you shield us from harm.
Do not grant the desires of the wicked;
Do not let their evil plots win against us.

Let those surrounding us with hate be silenced.
Let truth uncover them and evaporate their plans.
Let them fall powerless to their own revelations.
Let their own evil hunt them down.

America knows you God.
You defend the cause of the needy, execute justice for the poor, and raise up the humble-hearted.
Those who love you shall give thanks to your gracious and holy name.
The faithful shall live out their days with you.

Thanks be to God, our Redeemer. Amen

PRESERVE US FROM EVIL

I call upon you, O Lord; come quickly to me; give ear to my voice when I call to you.
—PSALM 141:1

Our Lord, Our God,

America calls to you in the night for your solace and protection.
Incline your listening ear and turn your loving gaze to us.
Accept our prayers as an offering to you, and our lifted hands as our repentance.
Let us pour out our hearts to you and release our suffering.
Let us hear your counsel and receive your instruction.

Help us watch our words, so our lips do not betray us.
Guard our thoughts that we may think in ways pleasing to you.
Ease our worries and concerns that we may simply rejoice in you with uplifted spirits.
Hear our supplications and our prayers Lord.
We pray for the grace of living according to your Word.

We pray continuously for your protection against evil deeds.
Let us not be seduced by the evil one's delicacies tempting our vulnerabilities.
Let us not be tempted by anything that is not righteous.
Let those who choose the path of self-adulation fall away from us, ensnared by their own evil thoughts.
Let the innocents caught in their self-destruction be released and forgiven to start a new day with you in the lead.

Our eyes turn heavenward toward you.
We seek refuge in you, do not leave us defenseless.
We entrust all our hopes and dreams in you.
Keep us steady on your righteous path.
For your way is the path of peace that begins in the hearts of your beloved.

How great you are, O Lord! In you we release ourselves fully. Amen

PERSECUTION NO MORE

Bring me out of prison, so that I may give thanks to your name. The righteous shall surround me, for you will deal bountifully with me.
—PSALM 142:7

Father of Sacred Deliverance,

When Americans lift our voices to cry out in the night,
When we make our requests to you, Lord,
When we pour out our complaints and tell of all our troubles,
When our spirits are faint, you know how to comfort us.

The fallen lay in wait to trap the unsuspecting on their paths.
The evil one insinuates itself into the minds of the vulnerable,
Causing them to turn away from the light.
They believe they have no refuge, and no one cares for them.

The evil-infected minds are without reason and justice.
They demonize and idolize people, totally wrong in their judgments.
Give vision and true seeing to your people Lord, and guard them from their vulnerabilities.
Let them not be seduced; attract them into your love-light.

Rescue us from those pursuing us, for they will overpower us.
Release our imprisonment, in heart, mind, body, and spirit.
Attract us to you and guard our whole being.
Guide us in the truth of your way, for you deal bountifully with your beloved ones.

Praise our gracious and merciful Savior! Amen

FREE OF THE ENEMY

Let me hear of your steadfast love in the morning, for in you I put my trust. Teach me the way I should go, for to you I lift up my soul.
—PSALM 143:8

Righteous Lord, Holy of Holies, God of Gods,

Hear America's fervent prayers, O Lord! We need you with us in this time of chaos and uncertainty. We are weakened, isolated, afraid, and alone. Who can we turn to but you, O Lord? Who will help us find solace and peace if not you?

The hidden enemy has pursued us, ignoring our borders, infecting our bodies, putting our people in abject fear. Our economy is crushed to the ground; our people sit inside tucked away from others. Our spirits are faint within us and our hearts are appalled to see the chaos unleashed on our cities.

We remember the days when all your tasks laid out before us: serving, caring, giving, saving, creating, loving, hugging, living, and worshipping. We meditate on the miraculous works of your hands. We are seeking after you Lord, as a deer seeks the river's edge, panting, thirsting, and needing.

Flee quickly to us with your answers before we fail. Do not turn away from us, for it's like being cast far away from you. Let us hear your voice speaking in your loving tones, morning to night. We place our full trust in you alone to lead us forward now, and to lift up our bodies, minds, and souls for the work ahead.

Won't you rescue us from the dreadful condition we're in? Won't you turn the tide to our advantage and end the evil plague? We know we can rely on your promises that you are there with us and your Spirit can teach us everything we need to know. Lead us on new paths of safety to live free again. Renew your promises to flourish your devoted servants.

Praise be to God the deliverer. Amen

NATIONAL DELIVERANCE

*Happy are the people to whom such blessings fall;
happy are the people whose God is the Lord.*
—PSALM 144:15

Lord God, Our Refuge,

Bless America, Lord. Train us to defend ourselves and stand our ground for the American Way. We stand strong in you, knowing you are everything we need. You are Lord of all and subdue all with your righteous bearing. You stand with those you love and ensure they live in your protection and safety.

Stretch out your hand across the heavens; set us free from the will of our enemies who seek to shut us down, close our doors, isolate our people, and make us afraid. Rescue us from the powers seeking our destruction; those building their case against us with lies and false accusations.

Liberate us to sing the new freedom songs of gratitude, to dance in the streets, to sit in our churches, to eat at table with family and friends, to do good work, and to rejoice in our blessings. Deliver us from the hands of the deceitful, and their lies. Teach us to love you, to love one another, and to do your will.

Let our daughters and sons have their full childhood experience. Let them play their games, learn your truths, grow up strong, celebrate each milestone, and love America. Let your abundant provision fill the shelves, the stores, and the stockpiles, made from America's hands.

Unite all Americans in your name. Let us cherish our life united as states seeking what's good for our people. May there be no lines of division, no slanderous rhetoric to ignite and divide, and no falsehoods scattered in the air waves. Let truth, liberty, and justice guide our every moment.

Happy shall we be when your blessings reign above all. Happy shall we be whose God is you, our mighty Lord.

Come and bring us blessings of unity. Amen

GOD IS GREAT

Every day I will bless you and praise your name forever and ever.
—PSALM 145:2

Wonderful God,

America exalts you on high, our God and our King, and we bless you, now and forever. Day by day, we praise your glorious name, from now to eternity. For you are magnificent God, and never will there be enough praises to tell of your greatness.

Generations shall tell stories of your wondrous works and declare how great you are! Morning to morning Americans meditate on the glorious marvel of your majesty and on your splendorous creation. We sing songs to your gorgeous light-filled heavens.

Night to night we give thanksgiving for your mighty and merciful acts, and your boundless love. We celebrate your abundant goodness and your long-standing righteousness. We headline the news of your unfailing gifts and awesome deeds.

We give you thanks for all your amazing works. Your faithful shall bless you and praise your glorious kingdom. They shall recount stories of your immense power for good and make known your astounding deeds. They shall hope in you always.

Your kingdom is from everlasting to everlasting and shall not be moved. Your dominion is over all kingdoms, and your supreme reign over all ages, generation to generation. Your rule is enduring and your power for goodness is immense.

You are faithful to your covenants and your promises. You are gracious in all your actions. You lift us when we fall and raise our heads when we bow down. Our searching eyes look to you, and you feed our bodies, minds, and souls.

Justice, kindness, and goodness define all that you do. You are always beside us when we call. Before us, above us, below us, around us, your love is vigilant. When we pray, you answer us. You never leave us when we walk in your truths.

Praise be to God in whom we trust, now and forever. Amen

OUR GREAT HELPER

I will praise the Lord as long as I live; I will sing praises to my God all my life long.
—PSALM 146:2

Merciful God, Powerful Sovereign,

When America cries for your help, you are right there.
When we seek your justice, you rule with righteousness.
When we seek your healing, you are the masterful physician.
When we don't know the way, you open it up before us.

When we become lost and confused, you whisper your solace and instructions to us.
When we are forlorn and bewildered, you send your consoling voice into the mouths around us.
When we are in need, you fill our needs with just enough, just at the right time.
When our hearts are broken, you hold us and cry with us.

When we are threatened, you guard us from evil.
When we are weak, you lift us up and strengthen us.
When we are belligerent, you calm us and give us right eyes.
When we are attacked, you shield us from harm.

No matter what Lord, you are always with us, caring for us, helping us, defending us, chiding us, directing us, and loving us.
Take our life Lord and create in us your masterwork.
For you are wonderful, our Almighty God.
We will praise you our whole life long.

Praise be to God, giver of all life, love, and grace. Amen

CARING FOR AMERICA

*Great is the Lord, and abundant in power; his
understanding is beyond measure.*
—PSALM 147:5

Almighty God,

Praise the Lord, America!
Lift your love songs to God for he is gracious and good!
The Lord builds America with his abundant power and strength.

With his hand, he restores our lives in more pleasing and prosperous ways.
He heals our broken hearts, bandages our wounds, and casts out contagion.
He gathers our isolated and lonely ones into warm and friendly places.

Praise the Lord, America, and worship his holy name.
For he strengthens you for the life he gives.
He blesses your children from generation to generation.

He grants peace from within your heartland, spreading out to your borders.
He fills your stores and storehouses with the finest provisions.
He commands good throughout your lands and within your halls.

He blankets our lands with the waters of heaven, quenching all thirst.
He instructs us with his words, statutes, and commands that we may live the best life he offers.
He gives us abundant and everlasting lives when we choose to live with him.

Glorious and generous Father, we praise your wonderful name.
Amen

CYNTHIA J STEWART

UNIVERSAL GLORY

*Let them praise the name of the Lord, for he
commanded, and they were created.*
—PSALM 148:5

Our God, Abundant Creator of All,

Praise the Lord of heaven and earth!
You created all living things and placed humans to steward your garden.

Praise our Father of freedom!
You created America to open freedom's gate to your beloved.

Praise God of all good!
You created us to explore your world and to enjoy it.

Praise the Lord of the dance!
The beauty and splendor of all creation praise your holy name!
... The twinkling stars...
... The brilliant sun...
... The magnetic moon...
... The roaming beasts...
... The swirling fishes...
... The chirping birds...
... The sunlit flowers...
... The rolling hills...
... The towering trees...
... The smiling babes...
... The humble men...
... The loving women.

Praise our Savior King!
When your creation was complete, you fulfilled your plan for redemption.

Praise the Ancient of Days!
America praises your name Lord and exalts you on high!

Praise be to God Almighty! Amen

GOD IS SO GOOD

For the Lord takes pleasure in his people; he adorns the humble with victory.
—PSALM 149:4

Lord of Victory,

Praise be to your holy name!
Glory to you in the highest!
Glory, glory, glory, praise be to God!

Your ends and purposes bring us into Zion, your holy place where all your faithful servants assemble as one great community of loving persons. All whom you created join in perfect harmony.

On that day Lord, when we join together as one, we rejoice. The sun is brighter, the moon is bigger, the stars are lighter, and the day is glorious. We sing, we dance, and we celebrate your holy name.

Our spirits are exuberant, and our love is overflowing. We embrace, we laugh, and we jump for joy. In you we have overcome!

All is complete in you Lord. We are one united people, with all your enemies turned to dust and their memory erased. We are healed, we are released, and we are jubilant!

O Lord, how great you are! How great you are!
Thank you, thank you, thank you for your abundant blessings!

Your blessings reign forever. Amen

UNSURPASSABLE GREATNESS

Let everything that breathes praise the Lord!
—PSALM 150:6

Gracious Lord,

America, praise the Lord for his surpassing greatness!
Praise the Lord in your souls, in your coming and going.
Praise the Lord for his abundant mercy and grace.
Praise the Lord!
All people and everything that breathes praise the Lord.
Great is the Lord. Glory to God on high.

Lift your hearts, lift your hands, lift your voices, tap your feet, dance your joy, and let all that you are praise the Lord.
See how great he is, all that he has done for you, and all that he has given you.
Be grateful and be gracious, for you have his love.
He has given it all and left nothing undone.
He has given it all.

Glory to the Lord on high!
Glory to the Lord everlasting!
Thank you. Thank you. Thank you, Lord.

All praise and glory are yours! Amen

YOUR FAVORITE PRAYERS AND PSALMS

PRAYING PSALMS FOR AMERICA

MORE PRAYERS FROM THE
HEART OF AMERICA

Volume 2
Inspired by Psalms 1-150

Cynthia J Stewart